Astronomy and the Bible

Astronomy and the Bible

Questions and Answers

Donald B. DeYoung

BAKER BOOK HOUSE
Grand Rapids, Michigan 49516

ISBN: 0-8010-2991-0

Sixth printing, September 1991

Printed in the United States of America

Scripture quotations not otherwise identified are from the *Holy Bible: New International Version*, copyright 1973, 1978, 1984 by International Bible Society. Used by permission of Zondervan Bible Publishers.

Library of Congress Cataloging-in-Publication Data

DeYoung, Donald B.
    Astronomy and the Bible : Questions and answers / Donald B. DeYoung.
        p.   cm.
    Bibliography: p.
    Includes indexes.
    ISBN 0-8010-2991-0
    1. Astronomy in the Bible—Miscellanea.   2. Astronomy—Miscellanea.   I. Title.
BS655.D44   1989
220.8'52—dc19   89-39
                                                         CIP

To my mother,
Florence,
and in memory of my dad,
John.
They first introduced me to God's creation:
planting seeds, picking blueberries,
watching lightning, and counting stars.
Their faithful Christian lives
have been the kind of example
so desperately needed today.

Contents

Part 3 The Stars

Part 4 Galaxies and the Universe

Part 5 General Science

Part 6 Technical Terms and Ideas

Foreword

Nearly three thousand years separate David, shepherd boy and amateur astronomer of Bethlehem-Judah, and Donald DeYoung, professor and physicist from Winona Lake, Indiana. What David knew about the magnitude and functions of the universe was almost nothing compared to the information available today. David lived in the "pre-scientific age" and thus was aware of only the sun, the earth's moon, four or five moving planets, and about three thousand fixed stars beyond. By contrast, as beneficiaries of late-twentieth-century scientific technology, Donald DeYoung and his contemporaries know vastly more about the physical properties and functions of the sun, the moon, eight other planets, more than fifty other moons, thousands of asteroids and comets, electromagnetic radiation, gravitational and other force fields, a hundred billion stars in our Milky Way galaxy, and the billions of galaxies beyond.

David may not have been technically knowledgeable about astronomy, but he was a wholehearted *believer* in his Creator and Lord. He was also a man after God's own heart (Acts 13:22). Even as a young lad, tending his father's flocks by night, David could intuitively relate what he saw in the sky above him to God's written revelation in Genesis 1. He wrote: "When I consider Thy heavens, the work of Thy fingers, / The moon and the stars, which Thou hast ordained; / What is man, that Thou dost take thought of him? . . ." (Ps. 8:3–4, NASB). He was totally committed to the proposition that God was the great Designer and Creator of the universe.

Tragically, in our great "space age," there are very few professional astronomers with full academic credentials who share David's faith. One of these is Donald B. DeYoung, my friend and colleague of nearly twenty years at Grace Schools, Winona Lake, Indiana. In his numerous courses, seminars, and publications on astronomy, he has clearly demonstrated that he knows and loves the God of creation, and takes the Genesis record with utmost seriousness. More consistently than most Christian astrophysicists, he interprets empirical astronomic data within the framework of God's special revelation in Scripture. Since God's Word is here given the preeminence, the reader may have confidence that the answers provided are not merely the whims of human speculation.

It brings me great joy, therefore, to commend this fascinating book to God's people everywhere. Such works are greatly needed in an age of dangerous and futile efforts to harmonize the perfect written Word of God with materialistic theories of cosmic evolutionism. May our Lord be pleased to honor this document for his own glory in the hearts of many people.

John C. Whitcomb, Th.D.
Professor of Theology and Old Testament
Grace Theological Seminary
Winona Lake, Indiana

Preface

One of the best parts of teaching and giving seminars is the question-and-answer time. The speaker never knows what to expect! Although some questions arise often and others are brand-new, all questions are encouraging signs that the audience is thinking. They also help to keep a speaker humble—because no one has all the answers! This book is a collection of many such questions from both the Bible and astronomy. My thanks go to astronomy classes at Grace College and also to audiences at Bible-science seminars. Their questions and interest have encouraged my own study of God's grand universe.

Astronomy books are difficult to write because one must keep an ear tuned to the news. New space discoveries occur continually, but some answers in this book are timeless, certainly true where Scripture is involved. I have tried to be tentative in areas where revision could occur, and any corrections from readers or questions for a later edition would be appreciated.

Most astronomy books take an evolutionary and secular view of science. They often raise more questions than they answer. This study attempts to bring some balance to astronomy by presenting a Christian perspective. Literal creation days and a young age for the universe are also promoted because I believe this view is true to Scripture and science. I have not tried to be artificially spiritual with the answers. Not all the questions touch directly on Bible issues, but the entire universe is God's creation, and all of astronomy proclaims this truth.

This book is intended as a resource for the classroom and home. The six "parts" are a somewhat arbitrary division of subjects. The final section is more detailed but is not just for technicians. Since many important astronomy questions are not addressed in this study, ideas from readers for future incorporation would be appreciated. Footnotes have purposely been omitted. Instead, references in the back are included for documentation of ideas and for further study. A short glossary with some basic astronomy terms is also included.

May this book help you to appreciate the details of the beautiful heavens as they declare the glory of God.

PART 1

The Earth and Moon

1. Is earth at the center of the universe?

It is popular today to deny any special recognition for the earth. Secular scientists tell us that we live on a speck of dust, circling a humdrum star in a far corner of an obscure galaxy! While this is all true, the earth remains of central importance. Scripture gives a refreshing contrast to secular thinking by declaring that earth and mankind are not an insignificant result of accidental evolution. The Book of Genesis states that our planet was created three days before the sun, moon, and stars. The purposes of the stars relate directly to the earth: to provide a calendar system (Gen. 1:14) and to declare God's glory to men (Ps. 19:1). The earth is also a universal reference point in that Christ came here to walk among men, and will one day return. An unseen spiritual battle goes on for the souls of men, focusing on this earth and extending to high places (Eph. 6:12). The earth is truly a spiritual center of the universe.

It was once thought that the earth was physically located at the exact center of the universe, and furthermore that it did not move. This "geocentric" view is still held today by a few people, although Scripture does not require it and observation clearly shows the earth's movement. The earth revolves around the sun once a year. It also rotates on its axis every 24 hours. These motions add together in a dizzy combination. The earth's spin results in a surface speed of 1,000 miles per hour at the equator. The speed of the earth due to orbital motion around the sun is 66 times greater still. This is 30 times faster than a rifle bullet. During an average human's lifetime (70 trips around the sun), 41 billion miles are traveled. While you read this page, the earth has already traveled more than 1,000 miles! Fortunately, we do not directly notice this motion since the earth's faithful gravity force ensures that both its atmosphere and inhabitants remain firmly in place. However, earth's motion is clearly shown by the westward movement of the sun, moon, and stars through the sky (see table 1).

We really don't know where the physical center of the universe is. If God's heavens are infinite in extent, then no center actually exists. But the question of the earth's physical position is less important than the spiritual reality of God's love for his people.

Table 1 **Earth's Major Motions**

Motion	Speed
Rotation on axis	1,000 miles/hour (at equator)
Revolution around the sun	66,600 miles/hour
Solar-system travel around the galaxy	500,000 miles/hour
Overall motion of the galaxy	1.1 million miles/hour

2. Did Bible writers believe the earth was flat?

No—this false idea is *not* taught in Scripture! In the Old Testament, Job 26:7 explains that the earth is suspended in space, the obvious comparison being with the spherical sun and moon. By 150 B.C., the Greek astronomer Eratosthenes had already measured the 25,000-mile circumference of the earth. The round shape of our planet was a conclusion easily drawn by watching ships disappear over the horizon and also by observing eclipse shadows, and we can assume that such information was well known to New Testament writers. Earth's spherical shape was, of course, also understood by Christopher Columbus. Some people may have thought the earth was flat, but certainly not the great explorers. Some Bible critics have claimed that Revelation 7:1 assumes a flat earth since the verse refers to angels standing at the "four corners" of the earth. Actually, the reference is to the cardinal directions: north, south, east, and west. Similar terminology is often used today when we speak of the sun's rising and setting, even though the earth, not the sun, is doing the moving. Bible writers used the "language of appearance," just as people always have. Without it, the intended message would be awkward at best and probably not understood clearly. When the Bible touches on scientific subjects, it is entirely accurate.

3. What causes leap year?

Leap years are needed in our calendar system because there is not an exact number of rotations of the earth (days) during one orbit around the sun (year). Instead, one earth orbit consists of 365 days, 5 hours, 48 minutes, 46 seconds, etc. Without any correction, "seasons" would slowly move through the calendar months, and farmers could not depend on the calendar for the planting of crops. March would eventually occur during winter, and August during the spring. Adding one day—February 29—to the calendar every four years makes up for the extra time, and this has been done since 45 B.C., in the days of Julius Caesar. However, even that extra day every fourth year does not entirely solve the problem. Since the extra earth rotation is not quite six hours, a new formula was established in 1582, during the time of Pope Gregory. Century years, such as 2000 or 2100, only have February 29 added if they are divisible by

400. Thus A.D. 2000 and 2400 will be leap years; A.D. 2100 and 2300 will not. This Gregorian calendar will keep the seasons assigned to the proper months for many thousands of years.

Why did God arrange for an uneven number of earth rotations for each trip around the sun? Perhaps because he doesn't want us to take the calendar system for granted! Throughout history the calendar has required monitoring and adjustment. Perhaps God is also showing us how important is every detail of his creation, not the least of which is the earth's motion.

4. Is the earth's magnetic field decreasing?

The ongoing decay of the earth's magnetism has been measured by magnetometers and satellites. In only 150 years, its strength has dropped by 6 percent, a dramatic change, especially on a long-age time scale. If this decrease continues at the present rate, the earth's magnetic field could disappear completely in just a thousand years. Without this field around the earth to shield it from cosmic rays and solar wind particles, radiation-induced diseases would increase greatly all over the earth. Perhaps the weakening field is an indicator that world history is drawing to a close. Scientists who think otherwise might well begin planning an artificial magnetic field made from superconductors!

Has the earth's magnetic field decreased uniformly since the creation, or does it have a more complicated pattern of change? This question is difficult to answer because we don't really know the source of the field. It apparently arises in the earth's greatest depths, about which detailed information is lacking. More historical magnetic data would also be helpful. Even assuming a recent creation, the 150 years of data mentioned above covers less than 3 percent of earth's history. At present, the limited data does indeed support a onetime decrease in magnetism. As such, magnetic decay is an evidence for a recent creation, on the order of 10,000 years ago (or less). This conclusion follows because there are limits on how strong the earth's field could have been in the past. Creationists eagerly await additional magnetic data, from either past records or present experiments, that will further refine our understanding of earth's magnetism.

5. Is there a hole in the ozone layer?

The ozone layer is composed of triatomic oxygen molecules (O_3) located in the upper atmosphere (12 to 18 miles high). These molecules provide an important protective shield against ultraviolet radiation from the sun. Ozone is very effective in absorbing the ultraviolet energy, and without such protection we would suffer from serious burning and a high incidence of skin cancer. A degeneration of the ozone umbrella has recently been measured above Antarctica, indicating that a partial opening in the ozone layer has developed. Whether the hole will grow larger or eventually seal itself up is unknown. It is also uncertain whether the ozone changes are caused by man or by natural processes. Although the effects of man-made chemicals such as Freon gas and jet exhaust are definitely destructive to ozone, it is surprising how tolerant to abuse are the ozone layer and the entire atmosphere. Given a chance to recover, these complex systems are able to restore themselves.

There is some indication that the recent degeneration of the ozone shield may be partially caused by the sun. Solar wind particles follow the lines of earth's magnetic field into the Arctic and Antarctic regions. The solar radiation may have destroyed or redistributed some of the ozone. If the sun has caused the opening, there may actually be a regular pattern of decreasing and increasing ozone over the years. As long as the ozone disturbance is small and remains limited to the polar regions, there is no great danger to mankind.

6. Has the earth's tilt changed?

The polar axis of the earth is tilted at 23.5° from the vertical. This "leaning over" is responsible for our seasons (see figure 1). Writers such as Donald Patten and Immanuel Velikovsky (see Question 30) have suggested that the earth's axis tilt was different in the past and that a catastrophic collision may have completely turned the earth over on its side. This event would have produced drastic changes in the climate. On the basis of this hypothesis, ice caps alternately pointed directly at the sun and then in the opposite direction. The earth's ice melted and refroze on an enormous scale, resulting in major flooding and animal extinction. Some of this speculation is used to explain the fossil record, the Genesis flood, and other Old Testament catastrophes.

Did the earth's tilt really change? No one can answer with certainty, but it seems doubtful, for at least three reasons. First, since the collapse of the vapor canopy is sufficient to explain the worldwide flood and fossil record (see Question 60), a changing earth tilt is an unnecessary com-

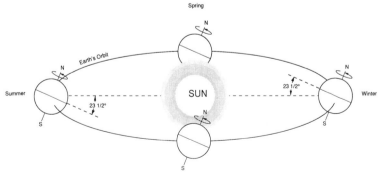

Figure 1
Earth's path around the sun.
Shown are the permanent tilt of the earth
and the four seasons in the northern hemisphere.

plication. Second, the regular seasons are cited in Genesis 8:22 as an example of God's faithfulness:

> "As long as the earth endures,
> seedtime and harvest,
> cold and heat,
> summer and winter,
> day and night
> will never cease."

Any shift of the earth's orientation would result in major changes of seasons. An increased tilt would cause more severe seasons; less tilt would tend to eliminate or reduce seasonal changes. Third, a temporary yet severe tilt of the earth's axis by a collision with some space object would have left permanent evidence, and that is not present today. For example, an elliptical moon orbit would be expected to result from lunar gravity interaction with a colliding object. However, the moon's orbit deviates a mere 12 percent from a perfect circle.

Many novel ideas have been proposed to explain unusual events in the earth's history. Some are incredible, such as the belief that the pyramids were built by beings from outer space. Other ideas remain as interesting possibilities, such as a changing earth tilt. The Christian who is interested in earth history should be aware of these options. However, it is unwise to give undue emphasis to purely speculative areas.

7. Is the earth's temperature changing?

Data collected over many years shows that the earth's average temperature has remained very stable. In recent centuries it has changed by only a degree or even less. A worldwide change of just 4° to 5° F would have major consequences. If it was a warming trend, the ice caps would melt and flood the coastal areas of the continents. Greenland and Antarctica would become newly uncovered real estate. On the other hand, a cooling trend would make living conditions in the far north and south even more severe than they already are. As the ice caps grew larger, ocean levels would drop and coastal shorelines would widen. There would be severe ecological consequences for every form of life on earth.

Some scientists predict that the earth's temperature will increase by several degrees over the next few decades. The cause is said to be the great amount of carbon dioxide that man has put into the air by burning coal and oil. The CO_2 could become a blanket that would trap solar energy at the earth's surface. This "greenhouse effect" is similar to what happens in glass enclosures, such as cars with closed windows. Even on a very cold day, sunshine will warm the interior of such a space. Other scientists predict an opposite temperature trend on earth since they believe that the sun may dim slightly and thus cool the earth. This happened during 1645 to 1710 and resulted in a period of cold weather over much of the world.

Which idea is the correct one for the earth's future, a warming or a cooling trend? Most likely neither of the opposing conditions will occur, and our stable climate will continue. Regarding carbon dioxide levels, the Creator has built strong controls into the earth's atmosphere that counterbalance the polluting effects of man. This is certainly not a license to pollute the land or sky, since all believers should have a great interest in preserving the integrity of the creation.

8. Is there a mystery about the Bermuda Triangle?

A strange area off the east coast of Florida gets a lot of bad publicity! Many planes and ships are said to have mysteriously disappeared within the so-called Bermuda Triangle. Sensational books have proposed that the lost city of Atlantis lies under the sea here—or that it is the site of an underwater flying-saucer base! As with UFO reports, a closer look at the Bermuda Triangle stories often reveals exaggeration or missing details. The most famous of these "mysteries" have common-sense explanations that are seldom heard. One interpretation involves the action of the Gulf Stream, which sweeps through that area of the Atlantic Ocean. Any downed plane or disabled ship in the triangle will rapidly drift northeast and thus out to sea, the result being an apparent disappearance of the vessel. The Bermuda Triangle region is a heavily traveled section of ocean, through or above which pass hundreds of ships and planes every day without incident. Whenever there is a problem reported in the region, another fanciful story quickly starts concerning "supernatural happenings." Of course, not every Bermuda Triangle mystery has been solved. However, commonsense answers will most likely be found.

9. What are meteorites?

There is a possible reference to a meteorite in Acts 19:35. Apparently an object that had fallen from the sky was worshipped in Ephesus, perhaps because this fallen meteorite was thought to be supernatural. Meteorites are rocks that fall from the sky. They come from the space surrounding our earth, a region that is a shooting gallery of radiation and high-speed particles. Some of this space debris consists of the remnants of old, disintegrated comets. Other material results from collisions between space material and the moon or nearby planets. Like a giant vacuum cleaner, the earth's gravity field sweeps up a path of this material as we circle the sun.

Most of the fragments are completely burned by friction in the 50-mile-high upper atmosphere. This results in

streaks across the sky known as "shooting stars," or meteors. They are not really stars at all, but instead are nuggets
of rock material, usually pebble-sized. The larger chunks
of rocks sometimes survive the heat and hit the ground,
falling at the rate of about a dozen per day. Meteorites show
signs of surface melting, and are either stone-like or an alloy
or iron and nickel. Most land in the ocean; the ones hitting
land quickly weather and blend in with normal rocks.

The largest meteorite crater in this country is in Arizona.
Half a mile wide and 600 feet deep, it was caused by a one-
mile diameter meteorite that probably disintegrated upon
impact, although fragments can still be found in the surrounding desert by using a metal detector. More recently,
two small meteorites hit a neighborhood in Connecticut.
One smashed a mailbox; the other space rock punched
through a house roof and landed in the dining room!

Several times each year there are meteor showers, occurring when the earth's orbit passes through a cloud of
rock material. During such a shower, as in a slow-motion
fireworks show, individual streaks of light cross the sky.
These showers are quite unpredictable in intensity. In November 1833, an intense shower (Leonids) occurred, with
hundreds of shooting stars seen per minute. A well-known
meteor shower called the Perseids, takes place around August 12 each year. There is about one meteor visible per
minute, with the best viewing after midnight.

10. What is a satellite?

In 1957, the Soviets put the first artificial satellite in orbit
around the earth. It was called *Sputnik*, and although it
burned up as it reentered the atmosphere after only three
months, this event launched the world into the space age.
Early satellites were watched by many people and observation times were listed in newspapers, but hundreds of

silent, graceful satellites now cross the sky unnoticed each night. Artificial satellites reflect the sun and look like slowly moving stars or non-blinking airplanes. Many move from west to east, while the polar satellites move in a north-south direction. The best time to see them is during the early evening, when a satellite may pass overhead every ten minutes or so. Some of them tumble in flight and appear to flicker off and on as they reflect the sun. Of the approximately six thousand space objects tracked by the government, two-thirds are known as "space garbage," such as dead satellites and spent rocket casings.

A satellite stays up because of its great speed. If it somehow suddenly stopped, it would fall straight to the earth's surface. Satellites circle the earth under the control of our planet's gravity force, like a ball swung on the end of a string. The Space Shuttle flies 200 miles high and circles the earth about once every 100 minutes, but more distant satellites have longer orbit times. The geostationary satellites, at a distance of 22,300 miles, take exactly 24 hours to complete one earth orbit. Thus, when placed in orbit at the latitude of the equator, they remain permanently over the same spot on earth. These synchronous satellites must travel almost 7,000 miles per hour to keep up with the earth's spin. They are equivalent to a giant radio tower that reaches into space, one-tenth the distance to the moon. You can tell where they are in the sky by looking at satellite antennae (or dishes), which are aimed at them.

One additional satellite should be mentioned. It is the oldest, largest, best-known, and most useful satellite. This object is the moon, our only natural satellite. At a quarter-million miles from the earth, it completes just one orbit per 29½ days (one lunar month). In comparison, all our space probes are tiny and insignificant. Man-made satellites are temporary, with orbits that decay sooner or later. What man sends up must eventually come down! However, the moon continues its 12 to 13 faithful cycles each calendar year, as it has done since the fourth day of creation.

11. Have scientists discovered the moon's origin?

Scientists have devised four major theories for the moon's beginning.

1. The *fission* theory states that the moon split off from the spinning earth, like mud flung from a bicycle wheel. Some say that the Pacific Ocean basin is the scar that remains from this loss of material. There are four basic problems with this theory. First, today's earth and moon do not have nearly enough circular motion for fission to have ever occurred. Second, although a moon split off from the earth would be expected to orbit directly above the equator, in actuality the moon's orbit is always tilted between 18° to 28° to the earth's equator. (This is the reason why the moon appears higher or lower in the sky during different seasons.) Third, while the moon was moving outward from the earth, gravity would have pulverized it into Saturn-type rings. Fourth, moon rocks are somewhat different from the equivalent material on earth.

2. According to the *capture* theory, gravity brought the moon into earth orbit when it once wandered too close to earth. The main problem with this theory is the low probability that two space objects would pass each other so closely. Another problem involves the actual "capture" mechanism: it simply wouldn't happen! Instead, the moon would continue on its journey. We have often sent space probe "fly-bys" to other planets and they are not captured, but instead are thrown outward with great speed, as in a crack-the-whip game. Finally, capture doesn't really qualify as an origin theory since it assumes the moon's prior existence.

3. The third theory has several names: *condensation, nebular contraction,* or *accretion.* It proposes the concurrent formation of both the earth and moon from small chunks of material. As a result, the moon "just happens" to circle the earth. The main assumption here is that the material would actually fall together into a big lump. Force calcu-

lations rule out such a collapse unless the cloud of material is already quite dense. Present-day dust clouds observed in space are nowhere near this dense.

4. The fourth lunar-origin theory calls for a *collision* between the early earth and another planetary object, an impact causing an orbiting cloud of debris that eventually grouped itself into the moon. Some critics of this theory believe that such a giant impact would totally melt the earth's crust. Others question the probability of another object's hitting the earth with the precise speed and direction needed to result in the formation of a moon. The main reason for promoting this idea is that none of the other lunar-origin theories works!

It was hoped by many experts that the *Apollo* program's manned visits to the moon would provide definitive answers to the lunar-origin question. Instead, many new questions were raised, and the origin of the moon remains a mystery to secular science. One common idea in each of the four "natural" theories is that the moon formed by relatively slow random processes. Scripture is in direct contrast to such reasoning—the moon was created suddenly (Ps. 33:6), from nothing (Heb. 11:3).

12. What causes the tides?

Oceanic tides provide an example of the moon's orderly and essential motion around the earth. Earth's tides are caused primarily by the gravitational action of the moon. As the earth rotates, the moon causes two high tides and two low tides on the earth's surface every twenty-four hours. Tides are especially high when the moon phase is either new or full. At these times the sun's gravity also contributes to the tidal effect. Even land areas rise by several inches due to the moon's gravity influence. The solid earth is somewhat stretchable and can be pulled out of its round shape by the moon's gravity. If we could only hear the creaking and groaning of planet earth as it responds to the moon's pull!

Surely ocean tides are not an accidental and random result of solar-system formation, for they have great value in cleansing shorelines and helping ocean life to prosper. Tides provide an important component of the ocean currents. Without these currents, the oceans would stagnate along the seacoasts of the world and the death of marine life— both animals and oxygen-producing plants would soon follow. Our very existence depends upon the moon's tidal regulation of this intricate food web. (See also Question 15.)

13. Why do we see only one side of the moon?

The moon rotates once on its axis during the very same period of time that it orbits around the earth: 29½ days. Thus, as it circles the earth, it turns in synchronism, so that we always see the same face of the moon. This is not unusual for moons; many other solar-system moons are similarly "locked in" as they orbit their planets. Our own moon has slightly more mass on its near side, so gravity keeps the moon turning with this near side toward the earth. The effect is similar to twirling a ball on a string. The tied side of the ball always faces inward.

It was not until the space probes of 1959 and 1960 that photos were taken of the moon's far side. An abundance of craters was found, but not as many smooth, dark areas as on the near side.

14. Is the moon "out" every night?

No—each day the moon rises about fifty minutes later than the previous day. This means that half the time the moon rises in the sky during daylight hours. When it rises in the morning, it is not likely to be seen at all! Table 2 shows some approximate rising and setting times for different moon phases. Israel's calendar during Old and New Testament times was based on these moon phases. A new month began when the waxing crescent phase (just after new moon) was first observed. Watchmen were assigned to locate this young crescent moon. Festivals were also scheduled around these moon phases (Num. 10:10).

Table 2 **Phases of the Moon**

Phase	Rises	Sets
New	6 A.M.	6 P.M.
First Quarter	noon	midnight
Full	6 P.M.	6 A.M.
Third Quarter	midnight	noon

15. Do moon phases affect the earth?

One obvious effect of lunar phases is the tides, which are highest when the moon's phase is either new or full (see Question 12). Many people also believe that moon phases influence the weather, agriculture, and animal physiology and behavior. In some cultures special efforts are made to plant and harvest crops during the "correct" signs of the moon. Both the changing brightness of the moon and tidal action may indeed have some influence on farm crops and animal life. Studies have also tried to find a connection between moon phases and such things as birth rates and incidence of crime. Some have gone even further and used the moon to predict stock-market activity. The results are not very convincing. Science can relate the moon's brightness and tidal effect to lunar phases, but some of the other effects, especially in farming, need more study.

16. What causes eclipses?

An eclipse of the moon occurs when the earth is lined up exactly between the sun and moon. The moon's phase must be full to move into this position. A *lunar eclipse* generally occurs once or twice each year, and the event can last for several hours. The eclipsed moon appears to turn a red-brown color as earth's shadow moves across its near surface. Alternately, when the moon moves between the sun and earth, a *solar eclipse* occurs (see figure 2). This happens at the time of the new moon phase. Partial solar eclipses can be observed almost every year, but a total eclipse is rare. It brings darkness to a small area of earth and lasts for only a few minutes. At this time the sun's beautiful corona, or outer atmosphere, can be seen.

It may seem surprising that our moon is able to cover the sun completely during a solar eclipse since the moon is almost 400 times smaller in diameter than the sun. However, the moon is also almost 400 times closer, with the result that the sun and moon have the same apparent size in the sky. Among all the moons and planets in the solar

Figure 2
Lunar and solar eclipses.
The positions of the sun, earth, and moon
are shown at the times of lunar (upper figure) and solar
(lower figure) eclipses. The dark areas represent shadows.
The figures are not drawn to scale.

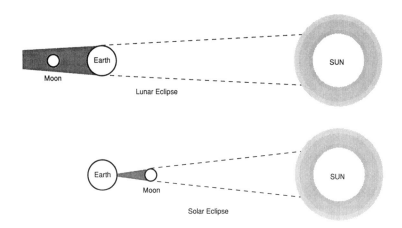

system, this perfect match only occurs between earth's sun and moon. As with all the details of God's creation, there is planning and purpose in eclipses. Since total solar eclipses are rare and very precisely specified in time, records of them have proved useful in assigning dates to events in history, including those recorded in the Bible. In an indirect way, eclipses serve as valuable "signs" to mark the days and years (Gen. 1:14).

A solar eclipse has been suggested by secular scientists as the cause for the darkness that covered the land at the Lord's crucifixion. However, this supernatural darkness lasted for three hours, much longer than an eclipse. It should also be noted that Passover was held on the fourteenth day of the lunar "month" (Lev. 23:5), which was two weeks *after* the new moon, one requirement for a solar eclipse. Neither could the Egyptian plague of darkness have been an eclipse (Exod. 10:23). The Exodus darkness lasted three days, and was probably more intense than that of an eclipse—yet "all the Israelites had light. . . ." One needs to resist the use of science to explain miracles!

17. What does a ring around the moon mean?

Although a ring around the moon could mean that rain or snow is near, keep in mind the uncertainties of weather predicting! A halo sometimes seems to surround the moon, especially during the full-moon phase. The halo is caused by cirrus clouds, which float three to six miles above the earth and consist of ice crystals. By day these clouds look like thin wisps or curls. At night they are too thin to hide the moon, but to us their reflection of the moonlight takes on the ring shape. Cirrus clouds often precede an approaching mass of moisture, which may or may not lead to precipitation. The next time you observe a bright ring around the moon, watch for a change in the weather!

18. What are the land and sky like on the moon?

Because the moon rotates once in 29½ days, the time between its sunrise and sunset lasts about two weeks. The moon's daylight temperature is around 200° F, with −200° F after dark. The bright regions on the moon's near side consist of rugged mountains and ridges between craters. The darker patches were originally mistaken by Galileo for oceans and still carry the name *maria* (pronounced mar'-ē-a), which is Latin for "seas." These regions are actually flat areas of basalt lava flows.

Since there is no atmosphere, the daytime lunar sky is very different from the earth. Air is required to scatter the blue color of sunlight across the sky. With no air, the moon's daytime sky remains as black as night. The sun itself is bright, of course, but its light is like a bright star in the night. The lack of lunar air results in no blue color or clouds, no colorful sunsets or rainbows, no wind or rain. "Shooting stars" never appear, because there is no air to produce the friction to heat up meteors. Occasional meteorites hit the lunar surface and make small craters, but there is no sound to accompany them. The stars and planets shine steadily in the moon's sky with no twinkling, although the same stars and constellations are seen from both the earth and the moon. The shift in position from earth to moon is not enough to make any significant difference in the stars that are visible.

From the vantage point of the moon, earth appears to hang motionless in the black sky. It shows different phases of light, but neither rises nor sets. From the moon, the earth appears four times larger than the moon does to us. When astronauts were on the moon, the earth's oceans made it look like a lovely blue oasis in space.

19. What is the "moon dust" problem?

The problem—at least for some scientists—is a *lack* of lunar dust. If the moon is ancient it should have collected a considerable depth of space dust, the material that continually rains down from space on to the surfaces of the earth and moon. Early estimates were as great as fourteen million tons of space dust falling to the surface of the earth each year. On that basis, there would be an estimated lunar-dust accumulation of sixty meters, in 4.5 billion years of assumed lunar history. On earth, dust is rapidly moved around by wind and water, with much of it being swept into the sea. On the moon, however, erosion is very limited and there is no wind or precipitation of any kind. The moon should therefore collect a growing depth of dust and meteorite fragments. The Apollo trips to the moon showed a thin (two to four inches) layer of moon dust. The astronauts did not sink into a deep sea of dust!

More recent measurements of dust accumulation from space give results as much as a thousand times less than originally thought. The early estimate of sixty meters of lunar dust thickness, divided by one thousand, results in only about two inches of dust, in apparent agreement with the long-age view. Two creationist responses will be mentioned. *First,* the evolutionary view predicts a much greater influx of dust in the early stages of the solar system. The hypothetical cloud of dust that formed the sun and planets should have been much thicker in the past. Therefore a thick layer of moon dust is still predicted, and it is still missing. *Second,* the revised value of a much smaller dust accumulation from space is open to question. Scientists continue to make major adjustments in estimates of meteors and space dust that fall upon the earth and moon.

Recent study of the problem can be briefly outlined:

pre-1966   Estimates postulated great depths of lunar dust.

1966   Unmanned *Surveyor* probes landed on the moon, showing little dust and a firm surface.

1969   The first manned lunar landing (*Apollo 11*) showed just two to four inches of dust.

post-Apollo   Estimates of dust accumulation were reduced. Another view is that the thick lunar dust is
actually present, but has been welded into rock by
meteorite impacts.

The "moon dust" problem has not gone away! The absence of lunar dust is an evidence for a more recently created moon than claimed by evolutionists. In view of possible
changing rates of dust fall, it is difficult to arrive at an exact
creation date from the dust data alone, but those that have
tried generally give an age limit of around 10,000 years.

PART 2

The Solar System

20. What makes up our solar system?

The ingredients of our solar system are:

One star (the sun)

Nine planets

Dozens of moons

Thousands of asteroids and comets

Millions of meteors

Since the sun accounts for more than 99 percent of the total mass, it is definitely a *solar* system. Pluto's orbit provides its outer "border," giving an overall diameter in excess of seven billion miles. A light beam crossing the solar system would require more than ten hours for the trip. Within the solar system, the planets circle the sun, and the moons in turn circle their respective planets. Gravitational attraction causes all the objects to move with clockwork perfection. The minor solar-system members—including rocks, dust, and ice—are also held captive by the sun's gravity force. Table 3 shows where the solar system fits into space.

Table 3 **Hierarchy of Space**

Object	Diameter
Earth	7,900 miles
Earth-moon orbit	239,000 miles
Sun-earth orbit	186 million miles
Solar System	7 billion miles
Milky Way	100,000 light-years*
Universe	30 billion light-years

*One light-year is about six trillion miles.

21. Has the origin of the solar system been determined?

The planets in our solar system are said to have originated either *from* the sun (fission), *independent of* the sun (capture), or *along with* the sun (nebula, accretion). Since these same three ideas also arise in current origin theories for the moon, the problems mentioned in Question 11 also apply to the solar system.

One version of the *fission* theory states that the sun was once sideswiped by another passing star and that huge chunks of matter were then torn loose from the sun and eventually became the present planets. However, a passing star could not provide the angular motion or momentum that the solar system possesses. *Capture* of planetary material by the sun is a theory even less acceptable than fission. Gas clouds are present in space, but one can hardly imagine their capture by the sun's gravity. Most clouds are very remote; they are isolated from stars by many light-years. *Nebular* formation of the planets requires that a gas cloud contract due to gravity and that the sun and planets then condense from the swirling cloud. There are two major problems with this idea. First, like a spinning ice skater who pulls her arms inward, contracting gas would have spun the sun up to a very rapid rotation. However, the actual rotation of the sun is much too slow to support this theory. Second, gas clouds in space are generally observed to either spread out or remain constant, not contract. For a typical cloud, outward gas forces are much stronger than the inward pull of gravity.

Since every secular origin theory begins with preexisting matter, none is really an *origin* theory at all! Aside from accepting supernatural creation from nothing (John 1:3, Col. 1:16–17), science must begin with material from an unknown source. Science alone will never have final answers regarding the true origin and purpose of the solar system. Only in Christ the Creator "are hidden all the treasures of wisdom and knowledge . . ." (Col. 2:3). This does not mean that we must abandon our search for scientific knowledge. It does mean that we must maintain a posture of reverence and spiritual humility in this search. After all, this is God's universe, and it reflects his attributes of perfect power, wisdom, and love.

22. Was the fourth day of creation twenty-four hours long?

According to Genesis 1:14–19, the sun, moon, and stars were made on the fourth day of the creation week. There have been many attempts to stretch the creation days into vast periods of time in order to accommodate Scripture with secular science. However, the problem is not with Scripture, but with our attempts to rationalize and understand the creation week, something that can't be done by finite minds! There are many details of God's creative plan that simply cannot be compromised with current science opinion. Some of the unanswered questions are:

1. How could plants exist on the third day, before the sun was present (Gen. 1:11–13)?
2. "Light" existed before the sun (Gen. 1:3). What light source did God use to mark the first three days?

3. Since the seas were also formed before the sun (Gen. 1:9–10), why didn't they quickly freeze? Why didn't the "water above" fall to the ground as snow (Gen. 1:9)?
4. Did the earth initially move in a straight line, or did it orbit the position of the yet-to-be-created sun?

An entire book could be filled with such questions from Genesis 1–2. All the answers would be speculative and probably wrong! The creation week was supernatural and therefore beyond our understanding. God had his own reasons for the particular order of creation events, and we are in no position to question them or to offer suggestions for improvement. *Yes,* I believe that the days of creation were literal twenty-four-hour time periods. Scholars have shown that this is the intended meaning of the text. The week of seven twenty-four-hour days, so familiar to us, had its beginning at the creation. God could have made everything in six microseconds or in six trillion years, but he chose literal days as a general pattern for mankind (Exod. 20:11). The literal creation days also display God's perfect glory and wisdom:

> Does not wisdom call out?
> I was there when he set the heavens in place . . .
> Then I was the craftsman at his side.
> I was filled with delight day after day,
> rejoicing always in his presence.
> Proverbs 8:1a, 27a, 30

23. What are the other planets like?

Let us consider a few distinctives of each planet in our solar system, in order of distance from the sun.

Mercury is the smallest and fastest-moving planet. It makes a revolution around the sun in just 88 days. Heavily cratered and without a trace of an atmosphere, Mercury looks much like our moon.

Venus has a surface that remains hidden beneath a permanent cloud cover. Some scientists once predicted that thick jungles and dinosaurs would be found on Venus, while others imagined a world completely covered by stormy seas. In recent years, space probes have ended the guesswork regarding Venus. We now know that its surface is covered with rocks, craters, and canyons. Any visitor would be poisoned by the carbon dioxide atmosphere, corroded by acid clouds, and crushed by immense air pressure equal to that of a half-mile depth of seawater. The visitor would also be cooked by the 900° F surface temperature and deafened by continuous thunder! Even though Venus is earth's twin in size, its conditions are the opposite of earth in every way. We can conclude that no Venus life has evolved, nor could life exist if brought there from our planet.

Mars has no canals, liquid water, or life of any kind. The sun reflects from its dusty surface with a yellow-orange color. *Viking* probes landed on Mars in 1976 and found a desert landscape. Mars has an extinct volcano that is three times higher than Mount Everest. There are also large canyons, one of which is four miles deep and sixty miles wide, four times the size of Grand Canyon. Mars has no air to breathe, and the evening temperature drops to −100° F. Beyond the orbit of Mars lies the *asteroid belt*, a group of many thousands of rocks that orbit the sun. Some are pebble-sized; others look like flying mountains. This debris is spread out over a gigantic ring that entirely circles the sun. It is not known whether the rocks were created in that form or are the result of some catastrophe in history, such as an exploding planet (which some scientists believe).

Jupiter is the largest planet, weighing as much as 318 earths. It circles the sun nearly half a billion miles beyond earth's orbit and has sixteen moons. A small telescope shows the four largest moons of Jupiter as bright dots alongside the planet. Two pink cloud bands on Jupiter's surface can also be seen. They are composed of a variety of poisonous gases. The weather report from this hostile world is not pleasant: magnetic storms, crushing air pressure, and cosmic radiation showers. Obviously there are no plans for a manned visit to Jupiter! Even if we could go, there would be no place to land, since Jupiter does not have a solid surface like earth. Instead, it is a sphere of thick, swirling gas, as are all the large outer planets. The most famous surface feature of Jupiter is the Great Red Spot. This hurricane-like swirl of reddish chemicals has been observed for centuries. It alone is several times the size of the earth.

Saturn, the second largest planet, is best known for its halo of rings, which are 160,000 miles wide and are composed of rocks and frozen chemicals, such as ammonia. There are actually hundreds of narrow individual rings, perhaps kept in place by small "shepherd moons" between them. Astronomers find it incredible that such intricate detail has remained in place for billions of years, although an evolutionary view of long ages leaves little choice. One moon of Saturn, Titan, was once postulated to have evolved life on its surface, since—among other things—Titan has an atmosphere and a large size. However, studies have found mostly nitrogen there, along with some poisonous methane and cyanide. This mixture produces smog and a surface temperature near −300° F. There may be seas of liquid methane and icebergs of frozen nitrogen on Titan, but there is definitely no life!

Uranus shines with a blue-green color due to its methane atmosphere. This planet has a dim halo of five narrow rings and is tipped over on its side. Miranda, one of Uranus's 15 moons, was studied by *Voyager* in 1986. Its unusual details caused one astronomer to call it "the moon designed by a committee"! Marking the moon's surface are great oval patterns of grooves, looking like furrows in a field. At Miranda's equator is a 12-mile–high giant cliff. Any astronaut who slipped off such a cliff would fall for ten minutes before hitting bottom!

Neptune, four light-hours out from the sun, takes 165 years for each orbit. A person born there would not live long enough for one Neptunian birthday. The planet's surface temperature remains around −328° F.

Pluto is the outermost planet in our solar system, circling the faraway sun in perpetual darkness. If this small planet has any atmosphere, the gases cover the ground as a snow-like coating. Future space probes will certainly reveal many more surprises awaiting detection in the far reaches of the solar system.

One conclusion from solar system studies is that its physical extremes are almost beyond imagination. The great variety in color, temperature, and surface details effectively rules out all of the simple, secular origin theories. Every scientific theory is based on patterns of regularity, but— beyond the basic laws of motion—each planet has been found to be unique and unpredictable. A second conclusion about origins relates to the lack of life on other planets. God has apparently chosen to place life on earth and nowhere else. And life has certainly not evolved anywhere else, either. The earth is truly to be enjoyed and appreciated for the many unique comforts provided for us. There is simply no other place quite like the "home" that has been created for us!

24. What are other moons like?

The earth's moon is just one of many satellites that circle the planets in our solar system. Pluto, too, has one large moon. Mercury and Venus have none, while Mars has two small moons that are shaped like giant potatoes. The other planets may have dozens each, and the known total for the solar system is now 57. This is an area of current research, and the number of observed moons keeps rising.

Space probes have revealed that each moon has its own unique details. For example, Jupiter's four largest moons illustrate artistic variety. They were discovered by Galileo in 1609 and have been studied closely in recent years. The moon *Io* is brightly colored in oranges and reds, with at least eight active volcanoes. Sulfur compounds expelled by the volcanoes have filled a doughnut-shaped region that surrounds Io's orbit around Jupiter. On Io's surface are lakes of molten sulfur, or brimstone, reminding one of the "fiery lake of burning sulfur" described in Revelation (e.g., 19:20). Jupiter's moon *Europa* is white in color with a flat icy surface marked by dark narrow fractures. *Ganymede* has a strangely grooved terrain, as if a giant comb has been dragged across the surface. *Callisto* is peppered with craters that are filled with ice. One giant crater on Callisto looks like a bull's-eye target, with ten outer rings of mountain ridges as large as the entire Midwest. The many planets and moons are not uniform in either color or surface features, as a common spontaneous origin might predict. Instead, each uniquely shows God's creative imagination.

25. Is there a tenth planet?

There is probably a tenth planet in our solar system, since the outer planet, Pluto, behaves as if the gravity of a remote object is pulling on it. This yet-unidentified object could turn out to be planet number ten, with still others beyond. Neptune and Pluto were themselves discovered by noting their gravity effect on nearer planets. Space-age exploration has verified the vast size of the universe and the infinite variety of created entities. Creationists assert that they are all made for God's own pleasure (Col. 1:16), including any planets in the solar system that are beyond the present range of telescopes.

You may have wondered about the names of planets. With the exception of earth, all are named after Greek/Roman deities. Any new planet will surely be named in the same way, since rules for such names have been established by the International Astronomical Union. It is a sad paradox that God's handiwork in the heavenly realm is named for pagan gods. The apostle Paul faced this same insult in his day. Acts 28:11 explains that Paul sailed to Rome on a ship that had as its figurehead, Castor and Pollux. These were Greek deities (as well as prominent stars), but the writer of Acts chose not to make an issue of this problem.

26. Do all the planets ever line up?

There was a popular idea in 1982 that the planets were about to become perfectly aligned in their orbits around the sun. It was predicted that this special situation would cause severe earthquakes and perhaps signal the end of the world. Since Jupiter is the largest planet, the event was called the Jupiter Effect. There was no factual basis for the Jupiter Effect story. No planetary alignment occurred (in 1982 the planets were spread over 98 degrees of the sky). The false rumor spread quickly, however, and will probably arise again in the future.

The nine known planets circle the sun at different distances and speeds, and occasionally two or three will appear to approach each other in a *conjunction.* Actually, of course, they remain millions of miles apart. To determine when all nine of the planets will gather to the same spot in the sky, one needs to calculate the least common multiple of their orbit times, which is well over a trillion years. In other words, all of the planets will *never* line up! Even if the planets did somehow align themselves, there would be no resulting destruction on the earth. Planetary distances are too great for one planet to exert a significant gravity pull on another.

Two lessons can be learned from the Jupiter Effect story. First, science cannot predict a date for the end of the world—"No one knows about that day or hour, not even the angels in heaven nor the Son, but only the Father" (Matt. 24:36). The second lesson depends on the first: false claims should never be used to bolster Bible truths, especially since Scripture does not need any supporting help.

27. How many planets are there in the universe?

This is an important question because life, if it exists elsewhere, could only be on planets or on their moons. Those who are confident that life forms exist in space propose that there are millions of other planets in the Milky Way galaxy alone. Actually, however, we can identify only nine planets in the entire universe at this time, all of which circle the sun. There may be many more or there may be none. Some nearby stars, such as Vega, seem to show surrounding gas clouds, but the observed matter doesn't really look like that of a planet. Barnard's Star shows a slight wobble in its motion, which could be due to either a nearby planet or to a companion star. Most of the other stars are simply too far away to detect any evidence for planets. Whether or not planets exist, one thing is certain: we have found no evidence that life exists elsewhere in space!

28. What did Halley's Comet teach us?

Comets orbit the sun just as the earth does. They are smaller than planets however, and usually have lopsided orbits which bring them close to the sun, then far out into space. Comet Halley has come and gone for this generation, and the reputation of comets was not helped by its poor showing in the night sky in 1986. However, it was known far ahead of time that the comet would not be bright. Apparently, the next appearance, in 2061, will also be poor viewing. The following visit, in 2136, will be very dramatic, just as it was in 1910, although that is poor consolation for *our* generation! The view we have of Halley during each of its trips around the sun depends on how close it comes to the earth. In 1986, the separation distance remained large, so visibility was poor.

Halley's Comet revealed much about itself to our instruments. The "head" was found to be a potato-shaped chunk of ice and rock, about nine miles across. When close to the sun, jets of gas and dust were released from the comet's surface. The "tail" of melted residue reached a length of millions of miles (there is plenty of room for such things in space!). By now, Halley's tail material has dissipated into space and its surface has shrunk by several feet due to the recent melting. It will soon be lost in the cold outer reaches of the solar system, just beyond Neptune—until its next pass (see figure 3).

Comets have given rise to many unusual ideas. Centuries ago it was believed that these "stars with tails" were signs of trouble on earth: wars, plagues, and the like. British astronomer Fred Hoyle recently proposed that comets

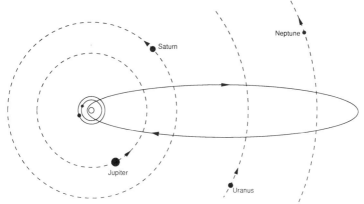

Figure 3
The orbit of Halley's comet.
At its most distant position the comet is three billion miles from earth. At its smallest distance from the sun the comet moves inside the orbits of Mars and earth (unlabled planets). The open circle at the center of the figure represents the sun.

are to blame for outbreaks of flu and smallpox. He believes
that comets, sometimes unseen, swing by the earth and
drop loads of germs on us from their tails. Hoyle assumes,
of course, that comets contain microbes, but—in reality—
life has been detected nowhere in the galaxy except here on
earth.

Comets may have a mixed reputation, but they silently
continue to orbit the sun and put on occasional displays for
us. Each year, dozens of comets loop the sun. Although
most of them have been named and measured on previous
orbits, seeing these comets usually requires binoculars, as
well as patience. Comets don't last forever; sooner or later
they are ejected from the solar system or melt into separate
pieces. There are clouds of dust in space that are the ghosts
of comets past. When the earth happens to move through
such a cloud, it sweeps up some comet dust. Then we see
"shooting stars," a repeat of the comet's original light show
(see Question 9).

This raises a very basic question about comets—why are
there any left? On a time scale of billions of years, they
should all be long gone, either by melting or by leaving the
solar system. The average number of solar revolutions before a comet melts is estimated to be about 40. Comet Halley has already been observed through 28 orbits, dating
back to 240 B.C. Its remaining years are definitely num-
bered! The Dutch astronomer Jan Oort has attempted to
solve this problem by postulating a great reservoir of fresh
comets that exists far beyond the solar system. He proposes
that a passing star disturbs this comet cloud from time to
time, deflecting new comets in toward a rendezvous with
the sun. With this cloud, the supply of solar system comets
is thus indefinitely renewed. At present there is *no* physical
evidence for such a comet reservoir, nor indeed any way
to verify its existence. Regardless, many astronomers have
a secular faith that Oort's comet cloud exists and that it
ensures a long time scale for the solar system. Perhaps there
is an alternative: the presence of comets may be an evidence

that the solar system is not nearly as old as is assumed by many people.

Halley's Comet teaches us three valuable lessons. First, comets provide us with a vivid object lesson concerning the rapid erosion and decay of the universe. All physical objects are temporary and fading. Second, God's heavenly handiwork demonstrates his infinite power and glory. Third, the exact motion of the sun, moon, comets, and stars is proof of God's controlling presence.

29. Did a comet kill the dinosaurs?

Some scientists blame comets for the lack of dinosaurs on earth today. They hypothesize that a large comet collided with our planet long ago. This resulted in great clouds of dust in the air, which shielded the sun and cooled the earth's climate for many years. Since dinosaurs could not adjust to the colder weather, they perished. This is just one of many theories about the demise of the dinosaurs. The list of suggested catastrophes, both on the earth and in the sky, is considerable. Some of the other astronomical events used to explain the death of dinosaurs are:

1. The sun became either too hot or too cold for dinosaurs.
2. The world's climate became either too dry or too wet.
3. A supernova exploded nearby, spraying the earth with radiation.
4. Earth's magnetic field reversed, and incoming radiation killed most life.
5. A passing comet poisoned the earth with chemicals.
6. A giant meteorite crashed into the sea, and a tidal wave then swept the land and drowned life.

There is a lack of supporting evidence for any of these events! Instead, creationists suggest that most dinosaurs died as a result of the great flood described in Genesis 6–8. Dinosaur types which were preserved on the ark probably faced severe climate changes following the flood. Creation research continues to demonstrate the importance of the worldwide flood in explaining earth's history.

30. Did natural catastrophes shape our world's destiny?

Immanuel Velikovsky (1895–1979) was a Russian-born writer, trained in medicine and psychology. He developed many original and novel ideas regarding the history of the solar system and mankind (see also Question 6). In particular, he believed that major catastrophes have shaped the earth and planets, thus challenging the idea that slow changes in the present are the key to the past. Because he went against the grain of current scientific opinion, his views were rejected by many people. Mavericks in science or in any other field often face emotional opposition from the establishment. Velikovsky wrote several books—including *Worlds in Collision* (1950), *Ages in Chaos* (1952), and *Earth in Upheaval* (1955)—and his popularity as an underdog has grown in recent years.

Velikovsky's ideas are most likely a mixture of truth and error. His proposal of a recent Ice Age is shared with Creationists, as are his challenges to "the doctrine of uniformity" (that rates of formation and erosion have always been constant). However, Velikovsky is hardly a friend of creationists or Christians in general since he accepts evolutionary theory and bases mutations on massive doses of radiation that occasionally hit the earth. Velikovsky denies the Genesis flood and attempts to explain away the Old Testament miracles as natural catastrophes. He made so many astronomical predictions that some of them were bound to prove correct. For example, he suggested that Jupiter must produce strong radio signals—and the signals were discovered a year later. However, Velikovsky also claimed that Venus clouds were rich in carbon and dust; yet Venus probes have shown this idea to be entirely incorrect. Velikovsky was a brilliant scientist and some of his views show good insight. But, although his writings are valuable for study, he was certainly as fallible in his thinking as the rest of us.

31. What powers the sun?

The dominant view of scientists is that nuclear fusion provides the sun's energy. Accordingly, hydrogen is converted to helium, releasing some of the vast energy stored in the nucleus. Along with heat and light, the fusion process should also produce a multitude of subatomic particles called neutrinos. The hydrogen-helium reaction is thought to occur at such a rapid rate that the earth is continually flooded with these neutrinos. Theoretically, each square inch of the earth's surface should be hit by a trillion neutrinos each second, day and night! These neutrinos, if measured, would be the best evidence that nuclear fusion is indeed occurring within the sun. *But here we face a major problem in astronomy,* since neutrino detectors do not find neutrinos in sufficient numbers to agree with this nuclear theory. As a result, some scientists question whether nuclear fusion is the real energy source for the sun. In effect, we are not absolutely certain what makes the sun shine!

The main scientific alternative for explaining the sun's energy is called "gravitational collapse" (see Question 99). That is, if the sun is slowly contracting, great amounts of energy would be released. Efforts to measure a changing solar diameter are so far inconclusive, but the chief argument used against the gravity source for the sun's energy is that the time scale required is "too short." Gravity collapse could keep the sun hot for only a few million years at most, whereas fusion could go on a thousand times longer. The long-age framework of modern evolutionary thinking has strongly biased the view of solar energy. If gravity collapse turns out to be the correct theory, the sun and solar system must be much younger than previously thought. Solar energy may also be due to a combination of gravity and nuclear effects.

The sun is an average star, the only star that we can study closely. And yet we do not really know what powers it! This bears testimony to man's limited understanding of his nearest neighbors, let alone the entire universe.

32. Is the sun shrinking in size?

A gradual decrease in the sun's diameter can be expected if solar energy is due to gravitational collapse instead of nuclear fusion (see Questions 31 and 99). A change of radius of about eighty feet per year would be necessary to produce the sun's actual energy. Astronomers have attempted to measure changes in solar size for many years, but the procedure is extremely difficult. Vibrations of the sun and month-to-month irregularities of the solar surface can mask the effect. Although present data does not clearly show a shrinking sun, perhaps eclipse records will eventually help answer the question. Meanwhile, the possibility of a slowly shrinking sun remains.

33. What causes an aurora?

Contrary to common belief, the northern lights—or *aurora borealis*—are not a reflection of sunlight off the polar ice caps. If this were true, we would see the lights constantly. Instead, an aurora is a form of radiation made visible. It begins with protons and electrons that are boiled off the surface of the sun. In a few hours these high-speed particles reach the vicinity of earth. They are potentially dangerous to our health, but they do not hit the earth directly. Instead, the earth's magnetic field deflects the particles and sweeps them into the polar regions. As this radiation hits the upper atmosphere, molecules of air begin to glow with energy. The northern lights often take the form of waving curtains of pastel colors. Some of the radiation is also sent to the Antarctic region, creating a display of southern lights (*aurora australis*). Since both the northern and southern polar regions are largely uninhabited, the radiation hazard to earth is minimized.

The further north one travels above the equator, the brighter and more frequent the auroral display becomes. The activity actually occurs in a donut-shaped region around the magnetic poles (60 to 600 miles high). The "donut" grows or shrinks according to the amount of incoming solar radiation. Canadians often speak of the beauty of the light display, and some say that the aurora seems to make a tingling sound on frigid nights. This type of strong solar activity can also affect worldwide radio communication.

The best chance to see an auroral display occurs about every eleven years (e.g., 1992, 2003), when the sun is extra-active in its production of radiation particles. For reasons unknown, our sun goes through a very active period on an eleven-year schedule. Then the sun becomes speckled with black blemishes called sunspots (see next question). There is also an increase in the number of solar flares, a form of surface explosion. Accompanying this activity is an increase in solar radiation. These details are all part of the complexity of the solar furnace.

34. What are sunspots?

When Galileo studied these dark specks on the surface of the sun in 1610, he thought that they might be openings into the sun's interior. Actually, sunspots are whirlpools of particles that are stirred up by intense electric and magnetic fields. The spots appear dark because they are 30 percent cooler than the rest of the sun's surface, although they are about 4000° C, hotter than molten metal.

Many sunspots are larger than the entire earth's diameter. They can best be seen by projecting the sun's image through a telescope onto a flat surface. Over several days the spots are seen to move across the solar surface, which demonstrates the sun's turning motion.

Sunspot numbers pass through a maximum about every eleven years. During this time the sun is covered with scores of spots, although at other times there may be none at all. The reason for this cycle of activity is not understood. The next good viewing of sunspots is expected to occur around 1991–92 and again during 2002–3. When at maximum numbers, sunspots have a number of effects on the earth. Associated with the spots are large solar eruptions called flares. These explosions eject electrons, protons, and ions into space. When they reach the earth, they cause an increase in the aurora, visible in the far north and south (see previous question). The particles can also cause radio-TV reception to skip over long distances. Magnetic compasses can be affected, as can telephone communications. Less clear is the connection between sunspots and the world's climate. It has been observed in the past that reduced sunspot activity seems to lead to drought and lower temperatures. For example, during 1645 to 1710, there occurred what is called the Little Ice Age, when worldwide temperatures dropped by several degrees (see Question 7). This time of severe weather coincided with a protracted period of sunspot absence. Similarly, the "dustbowl" years of the 1930s occurred during a period of few sunspots. How dependent we are on the slightest changes in our nearest star!

35. Can we explain the "long days" of Joshua and Hezekiah?

Joshua 10:12–14 tells the story of the day when the sun—and time—stopped. The Israelites were fighting the Amorites in Canaan. During the battle, Joshua prayed for the sun and moon to stop, so he would have extra daylight to finish the task. Scripture records that this prayer was answered: the sun "delayed going down about a full day" (v. 13). The very objects in the sky that the Amorites worshipped fought against them!

Several modern interpretations of the story have been suggested. Some say there was no miracle, but only poetic language. The Israelites had fought so hard that it just seemed like two days of work in a row! Others propose that a cloud shaded the sun, keeping it cool enough for the fighting to continue all through the afternoon. Of course, this relief from the heat would have benefited the enemy as much as Israel. Similarly, a solar eclipse has been suggested as causing reduced sunlight. But eclipses of the sun last for only a few minutes, not a whole day. All of these explanations fall far short of the statement that there has never been another day like the one described (Josh. 10:14; cf. Hab. 3:11). What *really* happened on that special day? As with all miracles, it is futile to speculate with scientific theories. The details are unclear, but we know that God could have refracted the light, or slowed the earth's rotation, or stopped the entire universe—all with equal ease!

Time stopped for Joshua, and it ran *backwards* for Hezekiah (2 Kings 20:9–11). God used this event as a special sign to show Hezekiah that he would regain his health. The sun's shadow moved backwards by ten steps, probably five to six hours on the sundial. That is, the sun appeared to move eastward instead of westward. The conclusion is again the same, that such a miracle is beyond scientific explanation. God may have temporarily reversed the earth's rotation, affecting all its inhabitants, or the miracle in Hezekiah's day could have been local instead of worldwide. The latter view is supported by 2 Chronicles 32:31, which describes envoys who traveled to the land where the miracle occurred. Joshua and Hezekiah both made lofty requests of the Lord, that the very heavens might be altered. And God answered their prayers. The sun, moon, and stars obey the Creator who placed them in the sky by the power of his word.

36. Have computers discovered the biblical "long days"?

The report that computers have discovered the biblical "long days" continues to be told *but is unfounded*. It is challenged here because false ideas should never be used to "support" Scripture. Furthermore, the computer story appears to raise modern science to a level of certainty that it does not possess.

As printed in tracts and magazines, the story describes a problem that scientists faced in the space program. Apparently a missing day turned up in the computer positions for the sun and moon over the past centuries. These celestial bodies were not quite where they belonged! The key to the problem was then found in the Old Testament. Mathematical corrections seemed to be needed for the "long days" of Joshua and Hezekiah (Josh. 10:13, 2 Kings 20:11). These events, when inserted into the computer, made everything turn out exactly right. Although this apparent verification of Scripture makes a very interesting story, computers are not this smart! The only way to determine a change in the sun's or moon's location is to know their exact positions *prior* to the change, but there is no such reference point available. We do not know exactly where the created sun and moon were first placed in the sky. Even eclipse records do not prove useful in solving the problem.

Can we not conclude that the long day of Joshua occurred exactly as described? And also that the backward motion of the sun in Hezekiah's time was a literal sign of God's power? Computers are neither needed nor able to prove these Old Testament events scientifically.

PART **3**

The Stars

37. What is a star?

The sun is an "average" star, so it provides a good example for descriptive purposes. The majesty of the sun is nearly incomprehensible. It is an immense ball of seething gases, 864,000 miles in diameter, nearly four times the earth-to-moon distance. If the sun could be hollowed out like a giant pumpkin, a million planet earths could easily fit inside, like so many marbles. But the sun is not hollow. Instead, an internal temperature of millions of degrees results from its furnace of nuclear reactions. (Note that I am using "nuclear fusion" to illustrate the magnitude of solar energy, but see Questions 31 and 99 for further discussion.) Hydrogen fuses into helium with a release of energy and a loss of mass. In the sun, trillions of hydrogen atoms must disappear continually. Since about eight billion tons of solar material are converted entirely into energy each second, the sun is losing weight, moment by moment. As a result of the process, each square inch of the sun's surface shines with the intensity of 300,000 candles. This incredible energy production goes on day and night, summer and winter. Only one billionth of the sun's energy output actually hits the earth. The rest streams off into all directions of space. In just one second, the sun releases more energy than mankind has produced since the creation, including all the engines, power plants, and bombs ever constructed. The dramatic energy output of the sun illustrates what is also happening at this moment on innumerable other stars throughout our galaxy and the entire universe. There is no energy shortage on the part of these beautiful lights in the night sky, "the work of [God's] fingers" (Ps. 8:3).

There are hazards involved in living as close to this star as we do. Along with the sun's pleasant light and necessary warmth, dramatic explosions on the solar surface also bathe the earth in radiation. However, we are providentially protected from harm by multiple levels of safety shields. For example, when x-rays and gamma radiation from the sun (the most deadly solar output) collide with molecules high in the earth's atmosphere, the radiation energy is absorbed and broken down to a harmless level. In addition, ultraviolet radiation is stopped by the ozone layer, twelve to eighteen miles above the earth's surface. High-speed fragments of atoms, also called the solar wind, are deflected by the earth's magnetic field away from the most populated areas and toward the far north and south regions of the planet. Finally, the 93 million miles that separate us from the sun also insulate us from harm. If this expanse were not a vacuum, the explosive sounds of the hot sun would deafen us. If the distance were less, the raging solar inferno could entirely vaporize the earth in an instant. The multiple safety features provided by God result in our safely enjoying the beneficial sunlight.

38. Is every star different?

Even though there are more than 10^{22} stars in the universe, each is unique. No two stars have exactly the same properties. This may sound like guesswork, since we have analyzed very few stars in detail, but the conclusion is a certainty. A star has so many variables in its makeup that the probability of two identical stars is zero. These variables include the total number of atoms, exact composition of elements, size, and temperature. Some stars show obvious color and brightness differences. Others require spectroscopic study to detect their particular identity or fingerprint.

Similarly, it is also true that every snowflake, blade of grass, and grain of sand is different. They may all look alike but they are not! On the microscopic level, there is practically an infinite number of ways to arrange atoms. Even a single snowflake, for example, has about 10^{20} atoms arranged within itself! Every individual object in the universe, no matter how large or small, shows God's creative glory and his artistry.

39. How many stars are there?

On a clear, moonless night about 3,000 stars are visible with the unaided eye. A small telescope would increase the number to 100,000. But this is just the beginning! The stars we can see are all in our corner of the Milky Way galaxy. This entire galaxy numbers about 100 billion stars. And beyond the Milky Way are other galaxies of all shapes and sizes. Around 100 billion such galaxies are known to exist. Taking the Milky Way as an average galaxy, the total number of stars is thus (100 billion)^2 = $(10^{11})^2$ = 10^{22}. The estimated stars number 10,000,000,000,000,000,000,000, when we write this number out.

Suppose these stars were divided up among the world's total population of five billion people. Then each person would receive two trillion stars! Yet all these stars may be only page one in God's catalog of the heavens. New instruments continue to probe deeper into space, with no end in sight. Perhaps there is actually an infinite number of stars. What an excellent way for the Creator to show his glory!

Whatever the number he has created, God calls all the stars by name, and he keeps count of them (Ps. 147:4; Isa. 40:26).

40. How are star distances measured?

Since radar and space probes cannot yet reach the stars, other methods are needed for finding stellar distances. Nearby stars are measured with *parallax,* which involves taking two measurements of the star's exact position in the sky. The readings are taken on opposite sides of the earth's orbit, six months apart. From this triangulation (or surveying) method, the star distance is determined. In figure 4, the parallax angle is exaggerated. It is always smaller than one second of arc, less than 0.0003 degrees. The parallax technique works for stars out to a distance of about 300 light-years (ly). (See Question 74 for the definition of a light-year.) About 700 stars fall within this range, including Arcturus (36 ly), Sirius (8.6 ly), and Spica (220 ly). Beyond 300 light-years, the parallax angle becomes too small for accurate measure.

For the longer distances, indirect methods are used. The Cepheid Star technique is useful out to millions of light-years. Since Cepheids are a category of stars whose actual brightness is well known, if a Cepheid appears dim its distance can be estimated. The method is similar to judging

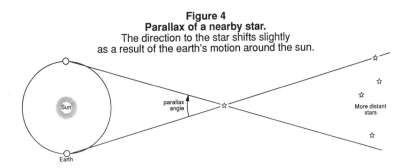

Figure 4
Parallax of a nearby star.
The direction to the star shifts slightly
as a result of the earth's motion around the sun.

the distance to an oncoming car by seeing its headlights in the distance. Cepheids are actually very bright stars, so they can be identified in other galaxies. This method gives the distance to the Magellanic Clouds (170,000 ly) and to the Andromeda galaxy (2.2 million ly).

The final yardstick for stellar distances that will be mentioned here is the red-shift of starlight (see Questions 63 and 66). This is a lengthening of the wavelength of a star's light as the star moves away from the earth. Most stars show this effort, similar to water waves stretched out behind a speedboat. The term *red-shift* arises because red is the color of visible light with the largest wavelength. Entire galaxies appear to be receding from the earth, as measured by their red-shift. The faster they are traveling, the further away they seem to be. There is considerable guesswork in determining actual distance from this red-shift, and there are also other possible explanations for the red-shift. If it is correct, this method gives distances for galaxies out to fifteen billion light-years. Astronomers also use several other distance techniques for stars. Although the parallax distances are accurate to within about 10 percent, all other methods are more uncertain. Actual star distances could be somewhat smaller or larger than current estimates.

41. How do we know what stars are made of?

Indeed, how can we study the stars at all? After all, it will probably be centuries before any space probe reaches a star. Even when viewed through the largest telescopes, all stars remain but tiny pinpoints of light, and simply cannot be magnified in size as planets can. However, each twinkling light carries a detailed message that astronomers have learned to decipher to some extent. Much as one can look through a glass prism to see the rainbow colors of light, careful study shows that every star bears a unique "fingerprint," or spectrum, in its light pattern. This spectrum reveals such information as the composition of the star. Most stars are found to be made of the common gases hydrogen and helium. The light from stars also reveals their surface temperatures. Some stars are just a few thousand degrees and show a yellow tint in the night sky. Hotter stars are blue or white in color and measure about 25,000 degrees. Starlight can also help determine the weight of a star, and the results are astonishing. Gravity has squeezed down many stars to such a dense material that a handful of stardust from some of them would easily weigh more than all the buildings and vehicles in a large city. One especially dense type is called a neutron star. If the five Great Lakes could be squeezed down to a neutron star's density, they would all fit in the kitchen sink. Of course, the twenty trillion tons of condensed water would be hard on the plumbing; it would quickly plunge to the center of the earth. Hundreds of dense white dwarfs (see Question 55) and neutron stars really do exist, but they are well removed from the earth. This is fortunate: if the earth were located near such a collapsed star, gravity would quickly tear our planet apart.

Additional information gleaned from starlight includes the motion, size, and distance of individual stars. Astronomers are kept very busy analyzing this constant flow of data. The Lord's creation is very complex, but he has given man the great insight needed to explore its rich details.

42. What is special about the North Star?

The most familiar star in the northern hemisphere is Polaris, the North Star. What is it that makes this star so well known? It is not the biggest star, nor the brightest, and certainly not the closest (its distance from earth is 350 light-years, or 2,000 trillion miles). What is truly unique about this star is that it does not appear to move. All the other visible stars move across the night sky from east to west and also change positions with the seasons. However, since Polaris is situated almost directly above the earth's north pole, as the earth spins the star remains in a constant position in the northern sky. On a long time scale (26,000 years for one complete turn), this alignment of Polaris with the earth's axis slowly changes. The earth's tilt remains the same, but its axis swings around in a circle (see figure 5). This motion is called precession and is due to the gravity pull of the moon. Back when the pyramids were being built, there was a different star above the earth's rotation axis. Passageways built into the pyramids were aligned with this previous Pole Star, called Thuban. During our lifetime, no movement of Polaris from its special position will be noticeable.

Polaris is an important star for navigation. From any location on earth above the equator, the angle of Polaris above the horizon determines one's latitude. For example, if you are at a latitude of 41°, the Pole Star will be 41° above the northern horizon. Early explorers on land and sea carefully used sextants to measure Polaris's altitude and thus determine their location. The sun can also be used, but the process is not as direct. Below the equator, Polaris is permanently out of sight. No convenient star lies beyond the

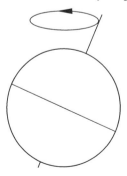

Figure 5
Earth's precession.
The circle drawn above the earth shows
the path of the earth's axis as it slowly changes direction.

south pole to help find one's southern location, an important concern to explorers. Today, of course, navigation is aided by satellite communication.

Recent studies have shown that birds, too, use the stars to navigate. During their annual migrations, many species of birds appear to orient their flights in the direction of various constellations.

Polaris is fairly bright and appears to stand by itself, high in the northern sky. To locate Polaris for yourself, the Big Dipper is useful. Two pointer stars in the "cup" of the Big Dipper lead the way to Polaris (figure 6). The Pole Star can also be seen at the end of the "handle" of the Little Dipper, although this constellation is difficult to see because the member stars are quite dim.

What actually is this pinpoint of light called Polaris? Measurements show it to be a fiery sphere, 1,600 times

Figure 6
Locating Polaris
The Outline of the Big Dipper constellation, also called Ursa Major.
The two end stars in the cup point the way toward Polaris.

☆

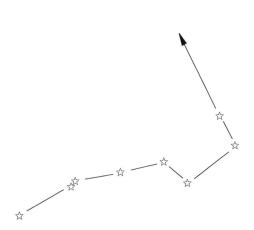

brighter than our sun. The brightness of Polaris changes slightly from night to night since it is an unusual type of star that expands and contracts like a giant bubble. If the sun did this, the earth's temperature would fluctuate by hundreds of degrees each week. Changes in the weather would then really be something to talk about! Fortunately, the sun is a star with very steady light. Telescopes show a second, pale-blue star that orbits Polaris, and there may be other unseen companions as well. The faraway Pole Star is a complex system that gives us only a glimpse of its beauty and design. The vast energy and distance of Polaris are beyond understanding, but not beyond appreciation.

43. Which is the brightest star?

The sun dominates our sky because it is the nearest star. However, there are distant stars that are actually much brighter than the sun. Consider Sirius, which appears to be the most brilliant evening star. This blue-white star is the fifth closest star to earth at 8.8 light-years, or ½ million times the earth-to-sun distance. It is also twice the size of our sun, and its high temperature produces the light of 23 suns. You can locate Sirius at the lower corner of a bright triangle of stars in the winter sky. The upper corners are formed by Procyon and Betelgeuse, stars in the constellations Canis Minor and Orion.

Sirius has had at least two other popular names. The ancient Egyptians called it the Nile Star, probably because it made an annual appearance in the morning sky in June, just before the rising of the Nile River. Sirius thus signaled the time of rejuvenation of farmland and also marked Egypt's New Year. Others called Sirius the Dog Star, and it serves as the eye of Canis Major, a constellation shaped like a dog. Roman farmers around 238 B.C. practiced the pagan custom of sacrificing red-haired dogs to Sirius during their festivals. This was supposed to prevent rust and mildew in the fields, hostile phenomena often attributed to Sirius in early astrology. More recently, some have thought that this bright star is responsible for the scorching "dog days" of late summer. Sirius is indeed in the daytime sky during August, but is much too far away to supply any heat to the earth.

Sirius actually consists of a pair of stars. There is a small, faint "dwarf" star that orbits the larger and brighter star once each 50 years and is affectionately called the Pup. The Pup is much more than a "pound puppy," since one handful of this dense star material would weigh 10 tons! About 1,500 years ago, the dwarf was most likely much larger than at present. It was then a "red giant" type of star (see Question 53), and eye witnesses recorded that the entire Sirius system had a red color. As stars age, many experience this shrinkage in size from giant to dwarf, with accompanying color changes. The changing Sirius star does not fit the pattern of those who believe in very long ages and slow changes of the stars, but the historical data cannot be denied. The Sirius star system demonstrates a rapidly changing universe and thus perhaps a much younger earth than evolutionists theorize.

44. What are "wandering stars"?

In Jude 13 the title "wandering stars" is given to false teachers. Leaders who lie lead people astray and are dangerous. Similarly, a literal wandering star is one that is of no use for navigation since it does not keep its same relative position among the other stars. Such "restless" night lights were noticed in Bible times and are today known as planets, a word that comes from the Greek for "wanderers" as used in Jude 13. Since planets circle the sun, they appear to move slowly through the background stars from night to night, spending some months in a particular constellation and then moving on. Planets are not usually placed on standard star charts because such charts would soon become outdated and misleading. We know that planets may look much like stars but behave very differently.

45. What was the Star of Bethlehem?

There have been many attempts to explain the Christmas Star scientifically, and three will be mentioned here. Some scholars think this "star" was a comet, an object traditionally connected with important events in history, such as the birth of kings. However, records of comet sightings do not match up with the Lord's birth. For example, Halley's Comet was present in 11 B.C., but the first Christmas took place around 5 to 7 B.C. Others believe that the Star of Bethlehem was a conjunction, or gathering of planets, in the night sky. Since planets orbit the sun at different speeds and distances, they occasionally seem to approach each other closely. However, multiple planets do not look like a single light source, as described in Scripture. Also, planetary alignments are rather frequent and therefore not that unusual. There *was* a conjunction of Jupiter and Saturn in 6 B.C., but an even closer gathering in 66 B.C., much too early! Finally, an exploding star, or supernova, has been proposed to explain the Christmas Star. Some stars are unstable and explode with a bright blaze. However, historical records do not indicate a supernova at the time of the Lord's birth. (See Question 54 on "supernovas.")

All three explanations for the Star of Bethlehem fall short of the nativity story as predicted in Numbers 24:17 and recorded in Matthew 2:1–12. Two details in Matthew are of special interest. First, the text implies that only the Magi saw the star. Comets, conjunctions, and exploding stars would be visible to everyone on earth. Second, the star went before the Magi and led them from Jerusalem to Bethlehem. This is a distance of about six miles, in a direction from north to south. However, not only does every *natural* object in the sky move from east to west due to the earth's rotation, but it is difficult to imagine how a natural light could lead the way to a particular house.

The conclusion is that the Star of Bethlehem cannot be explained by science! It was a temporary and supernatural light. After all, was not the first Christmas a time of miracles? God has often used special, heavenly lights to guide his people, such as the glory that filled the tabernacle (Exod. 40:34–38) and the temple (1 Kings 8:10) and that shone upon the apostle Paul (Acts 9:3). Such visible signs of God's presence are known as the Shekinah Glory, or dwelling place of God. This special light is a visible manifestation of divine majesty. The great mystery of the first Christmas is not the origin of its special star. It is the question of why the Magi were chosen to follow the light to the Messiah, and why we are given the same invitation today.

46. What is the Morning Star?

"Morning Star" is a name often used to describe the planet Venus. For part of each year Venus rises in the eastern sky, just before the sun. Since it is a very bright planet and at that time remains visible into the morning hours, it might be called a *morning* star even though it isn't really a star at all. During other parts of the year, Venus becomes an *evening* star. Then it sets in the west, after the sun. Whether visible in the morning or evening, Venus never moves very far from the sun because it is an inner planet. Mercury also qualifies as a morning and evening light, but it is more difficult to see.

In Scripture the title *morning star* is used in three different ways. First, Job 38:7 describes angels as morning stars (or day stars) that sang together at the creation of the universe. Angels were part of the initial creation (Col. 1:16) and thus became witnesses of the great event. Second, the king of Babylon is described as a morning star and also a fallen star (Isa. 14:4, 12). The evil leader fell from the highest

position to the lowest, just as Satan did. Third, the Lord
Jesus is described as "the bright Morning Star" (Rev. 22:16),
which rises in our hearts (2 Peter 1:19). Early-morning stargazers often watch the eastern sky to see the brilliant planet
Venus rise to signal a new day. As Christians—children of
God—we are told to shine "like stars in the universe" (Phil.
2:15).

47. What are the Pleiades?

The beautiful group of stars known as the Pleiades is
mentioned three times in Scripture. Job 9:8–9 and Amos
5:8 explain their origin, stating that the Creator "stretches
out the heavens" and is the Maker of the Pleiades. Job
38:31–32 further declares that only the Lord can "bind the
beautiful Pleiades" and bring them forth in their season.
These stars are indeed gravitationally bound together in a
cluster. They appear in the November skies and are located
above Orion's left shoulder, where six icy-blue stars can be
seen in the shape of a little dipper, smaller than the moon.
Binoculars reveal dozens of additional stars in the Pleiades
group. The stars are 400 light-years away but are actually
near-neighbors of earth in the Milky Way galaxy.

The Pleiades stars have been described in many different
ways. Chinese records from 2357 B.C. describe them as
golden bees or flying pigeons. The Greeks named the stars
the "seven sisters." Early Russian literature pictures the
Pleiades as a mother hen with her chicks. For a while during the 1800s, it was thought that the Pleiades were located
at the exact center of the universe since measurements
seemed to show that all the other stars moved around
Pleiades. Today we know that the Pleiades group also moves;
it is actually speeding away from the earth at 16,000 miles
per hour. (See also Question 48.)

48. What do we know about the stars named in Scripture?

Table 4 shows where stars and constellations are mentioned in Scripture.

Pleiades This small patch of icy-blue stars appears in the winter sky. These stars are 400 light-years away, and are near neighbors of the sun in the Milky Way galaxy. As previously mentioned (Question 47), in the 1800s it was thought that the Pleiades star cluster was located at the exact center of the universe because measurements had shown that all other stars seemed to move around Pleiades. Today we know that the Pleiades cluster itself also moves. We also know that the center of the universe has not been found! The Job 9 reference explains the origin of these stars, stating that the Creator stretches out the heavens, and makes the Pleiades.

Bear and Cubs The Big and Little Dippers are known as the Bear and her Cubs (Ursa Major and Minor). The bright component stars are located prominently in the northern sky. They are circumpolar stars that never set, as seen from northern latitudes. The King James Version of Scripture translates the Hebrew name as Arcturus. The star called Arcturus is positioned today in the summer constellation Bootes, some distance from the dipper stars.

Orion The Hunter constellation dominates the winter sky each year. Since it is positioned directly above the earth's

Table 4 **Stars and Constellations in Scripture**

	Job 9:9	Job 38:31–32	Amos 5:8	Acts 28:11
Pleiades	*	*	*	
Bear and her Cubs	*	*		
		*		
Orion	*	*	*	
Castor and Pollux				*

equator, Orion is easily seen by people everywhere. Its two main stars, Rigel and Betelgeuse, are the seventh and twelfth brightest stars in the entire night sky. The Job 38 reference declares that God alone can hold together the stars of the Pleiades and Orion constellations.

Castor and Pollux Part of the Gemini constellation, in ancient times these two stars were thought to be guardians of sailors. In Roman mythology, Castor was a horse trainer and his twin brother, Pollux, a boxer. On Paul's final journey to Rome, his ship sailed under the figurehead of Castor and Pollux (Acts 28:11).

49. Is the gospel spelled out in the stars?

It has long been thought that the constellations are God-given illustrations of gospel truths. Indeed, constellation names go far back into mankind's history. The Jewish historian Josephus says they were named by Seth, the third son of Adam, but perhaps even Adam had a part, since he named the animal world (Gen. 2:19). The Bible says that God assigned his own names to the stars (Ps. 147:4). If so, he may have taught them to early peoples.

Of special interest are the twelve zodiac constellations. This band of stars lies in the plane of the solar system. They appear high in the night sky, roughly along the same path traveled by the sun during the day. During the course of each year the zodiac constellations take turns in appearing: for example, Scorpius in summer, Gemini in winter. Job 38:32 makes reference to the bringing forth of the constellations (or "Mazzaroth" in KJV) in their season.

The idea of seeing the gospel message in the stars was popularized by the writings of E. W. Bullinger and J. A. Seiss during the 1800s. According to this theory, Table 5 is a brief outline of the usual zodiac interpretations.

Early writings on this subject went into great detail on

Table 5 **Zodiac Interpretations**

Constellation	Picture	Interpretation
Virgo	Virgin	Virgin Mary
Libra	Scales	Sin must be paid for
Scorpius	Scorpion	Sin brings death
Sagittarius	Archer	Demonism
Capricorn	Goat-fish	Earth corruption
Aquarius	Water pourer	Living water or Noah's flood
Pisces	Fish	God's remnant
Aries	Ram	Sacrifice
Taurus	Bull	Resurrection
Gemini	Twins	Christ's dual nature
Cancer	Crab	Gathering of redeemed
Leo	Lion	The King

different parts of the constellations, so that practically every star was assigned a special meaning.

The gospel message may well have been purposely written in the skies by the Lord. In that case, perhaps the star signs served a purpose as memory aids before Scripture was available. Today, of course, the Word provides a clear message about the plan of God. Although stars continue to "declare the glory of God" (Ps. 19:1) and are useful in our calendar system (Gen. 1:14), the Bible does not tell us to search the stars for detailed messages. On the contrary, warnings are given against trusting in the stars. Caution is needed when searching for the gospel in the stars, since constellation symbols can have many possible interpretations. Since Babylonian times, Satan has counterfeited the zodiac with astrology.

Many people still claim to see symbols of the gospel in unusual places: crosses on flower petals, Christmas stars on sand dollars, and even religious images on rusty water towers! God certainly designed all things, but we must beware of building our doctrine on the details of nature. We can be thankful that the Bible presents the gospel to us so clearly that we have no need for additional evidence of its truths.

50. Did the stars fight against Sisera?

Judges 4 tells of the defeat of Sisera, a Canaanite military leader who fought against Israel, the Lord's chosen people, but lost his entire army as well as his own life. Judges 5 is the victorious song of Deborah, the prophetess who led Israel at this time, and verse 20 declares that the battle with Sisera was a heavenly one: "From the heavens the stars fought, from their courses they fought against Sisera." This is a poetic way of saying that the powers of heaven fought on Israel's behalf. The Lord and his host of angels assured the defeat of the Canaanites. Those who oppose God's plans have no more chance of success than if they opposed the motion of the stars above.

51. What is a black hole in space?

Black holes are invisible, weigh billions of tons, and are smaller than a kernel of corn! They have recently been made popular by science-fiction movies and video games, but black holes were first postulated by the French astronomer Pierre Laplace two hundred years ago. He realized that stars must collapse when they run short of fuel. If a star is heavy enough, there should be no limit to its contraction. It will first shrink to the size of the moon, then the size of a basketball. Finally it will have no size at all, as gravity crushes the entire star into a mathematical point. The only meaningful size reference is a "twilight zone" region around the collapsed star, possibly extending outward for millions of miles. Anything entering this region could not possibly withstand the inward gravity pull of the collapsed star. Even light cannot escape, hence the name "black hole."

Although black holes cannot be seen directly, there are ways to detect them in space since they should affect nearby stars, possibly tearing them apart and producing x-rays in the process. One likely place for a black hole is in the constellation Cygnus (the Swan), also known as the Northern Cross. The suspected region is called Cygnus X-1, a strong source of x-ray radiation. These x-rays do not harm us on earth but are readily measured by satellites.

Cygnus X-1 may be a black hole—or it may be some other unusual star. Except in movies, no black holes have yet been positively identified. Some recent theories in physics conclude that "black hole" stars are not stable. If this is true, they eventually evaporate into other kinds of matter. For the Christian, it doesn't really matter since—if black holes indeed exist—they are evidence for the decay of the universe. A black hole is, after all, a collapsed star, yet another phenomenon that illustrates the unending variety of created objects in the sky.

Some Christians have speculated that black holes might be God's energy reservoirs, needed for the future formation of the "new heaven and new earth." Black holes certainly contain vast energy, as does every star. However, energy reservoirs are hardly needed by the One who spoke the universe into being by the power of his word.

52. What is the Death Star?

Some scientists speculate that the sun has an unseen companion star whose orbit brings it close to the solar system about once every 40 million years. On each trip inward, this star unleashes numerous comets from the Oort Cloud (see Question 28). According to this theory, on a previous pass (about 60 million years ago), many of these comets hit the earth. This resulted in explosive collisions that pushed a great dark cloud of dust into the upper atmosphere and thus shielded the earth's surface from sunlight for many years. Since plants could not grow, the vegetarian dinosaurs starved, and the broken food chain soon affected the carnivorous animals as well. Geologists call this the Cretaceous extinction.

The star that supposedly started all this is appropriately named Nemesis—the Death Star—after the Greek goddess of punishment. The search for this disturbing star has been unsuccessful. Perhaps the reason is that the star does not exist! Creationists have a more credible explanation for the period of widespread destruction, based on the Genesis flood. It is interesting to note that the disappearance of the dinosaurs has forced scientists to postulate many world-wide catastrophies. They have abandoned James Hutton's "uniformitarianism," whereby all changes on earth are slow, and the present is the key to the past. The creationist position has always emphasized the role of catastrophies in earth's history.

53. Which are the largest stars?

There are indeed some giants in the sky! The largest stars are called *red giants* or super-giants. Their diameters reach more than five hundred times that of our sun. If such a super-giant star could be positioned at the center of the solar system, the four inner planets, including earth, would be vaporized beneath its surface. These giant stars generally have a red appearance due to their relatively "cool" surface temperature, around 5000° F. The following is a list of some well-known red giants, in order of increasing size: 1. *Arcturus* is a yellow-red star, the fourth brightest in the sky. It is twenty times larger than the sun. Arcturus is sometimes called Job's Star, due to its possible mention in Job 9:9 and 38:32. As a publicity stunt, light from Arcturus was used to trigger the opening of the Chicago "Century of Progress" Exposition in 1933. As the star moved in front of a carefully placed telescope, it triggered a light-sensitive switch. Arcturus was chosen because it was thought to be 40 light-years away, so its light had actually left the star at the time of a previous fair in Chicago, in 1893. More recently, the distance to Arcturus has been measured at 36 light years.

2. *Aldebaran* is the eye of Taurus (the Bull). Red giants make bright eyes for constellations! Aldebaran is about 70 light-years away, and is 40 solar diameters in size. This bright star is occasionally covered up, or occulted, by the moon.

3. *Antares* is an orange-red star, the eye of the Scorpion constellation. The name means "rival of Mars," which describes the star's planet-like appearance. Antares has a diameter that is 700 times the size of the sun and shines with the brightness of 9,000 suns.

4. *Betelgeuse* is the right shoulder of Orion (the Hunter). The diameter of this giant star is 1,200 times that of the sun. Betelgeuse gives off 120,000 times as much light energy as the sun.

54. What is a supernova?

A supernova marks a violent star explosion. As certain heavy stars suddenly become unstable in their energy production, the outer layers of star material are blown outward with tremendous force. For a period of months the star becomes very bright, giving off as much light as an entire galaxy of stars. Then the light slowly fades, leaving behind a cloud of debris that slowly spreads out over the centuries. The cloud is called a *nebula* and may be trillions of miles across. The core of the original star may remain in the midst of the cloud, spinning rapidly as a *pulsar* star.

One famous supernova was observed by Chinese astronomers in 1054 A.D. The star explosion was as bright as Venus in the night sky and, some months later, could be seen during the day. The Crab Nebula remains today at the site of this explosion. A supernova is a rare event. The last one in the Milky Way was recorded by Kepler and Galileo in 1604, nearly four centuries ago. In 1987, a more distant supernova made headlines when observed in the Large Magellanic Cloud, a neighboring galaxy that lies 170,000 light-years away.

A supernova is part of the aging process of heavy stars. It is yet another reminder that the physical universe is temporary.

55. Do stars evolve?

Some of what astronomers describe as "stellar evolution" does take place. However, the process is misnamed, and parts of it are questionable. According to this theory, the life of a star is said to begin with the collapse of a gas cloud—a doubtful beginning, as explained in Question 56. Bypassing this fundamental origin problem, a young star is said to begin in the "main sequence" category (see Question 98). These are average stars with a stable light output. The great majority of stars are in the main sequence, including our sun. When a star's hydrogen fuel runs low, it becomes a *red giant* or super-giant star. Such a star has expanded hundreds of times in size and has become somewhat cooler. Red giants include Betelgeuse and Aldebaran. Next, the star may either explode as a *supernova* or may slowly collapse into a small, hot *white dwarf* star. The companion star circling Sirius is such a dwarf (see Question 43). Such stars are said to be very old.

Notice that the entire life of a star is an aging process: main sequence—red giant—white dwarf. Instead of stellar evolution, it might better be called stellar decay, degradation, or degeneration. Computer studies conclude that each stage of a star lasts for millions or billions of years (depending on the star's mass), but—in the recent-creation view—there has not been enough time for such change. And some observed star changes appear to be much more rapid than computer models suggest! For example, there is evidence that the dwarf companion of Sirius formed from a red giant in just 1,000 years. Other stars have also shown unexpected color changes, indicating that the aging process of some stars may be much more rapid than generally believed. Most stars have probably not changed substantially in appearance since the creation described in Genesis. The sun has certainly remained as a faithful "main sequence" star from the beginning. Since all the stars were made on the fourth day (Gen. 1:16–19), they are all actually the same age. From the beginning they have differed from each other in color and brightness—"in splendor" (1 Cor. 15:41).

56. Do new stars form today?

The birth of a star has never been observed. The principles of physics demand some special conditions that make star formation very rare—if it occurs at all! A cloud of hydrogen gas must be compressed to a sufficiently small size so that gravity dominates. (As an example, the sun is a stable sphere of gas.) In space, however, almost every gas cloud is light-years in size, hundreds of times greater than the critical size needed for a stable star. As a result, outward gas pressures cause these clouds to spread out further, not contract.

A number of mechanisms have been proposed to explain the beginning of star formation. Most popular is a pressure or density wave in space, which might squeeze dust clouds down to star-forming size. This pressure wave is suggested to originate from a nearby supernova or exploding star. The net result of this reasoning is that stars are said to form from other stars. But where do the first stars come from in this circular reasoning? Another problem for this theory of stellar origins is the great distance between stars. Most are isolated from each other by ten light-years or more and thus would appear unable to influence each other's origin in any way.

Scientists point to certain areas where they believe stars

may be forming today. One of these rare spots is the Orion Nebula, a glowing gas cloud in the northern December sky. The infrared radiation emitted from this cloud is thought to be perhaps related to the start-up energy from new stars. However, there is too much gas and dust to see these stars, and the source of this infrared radiation may actually be a type of star that has existed in the gas cloud for a long time. All assumptions regarding present-day star formation remain speculative.

The creationist also sees a time-scale problem with theories about present-day star formation. Although computer models typically give a million-year start-up time for new stars, such unlimited time is not available in a "young" universe. Observations of space reveal the universal trend of star degeneration, not star formation. Star decay is a fairly common event in the form of novas and supernovas. Once again we can conclude that the universe of *created* stars is slowly dying.

57. Are we made of stardust?

This is the rather simplistic conclusion of the Big Bang theory (see Question 64), whereby the original chemical elements of the early universe are thought to be limited to hydrogen and helium. According to this secular view, all the other elements, now numbering 109, were later formed by nuclear reactions within the cores of stars. When these stars eventually became supernovae, the explosions spread their many elements far and wide throughout space. The solar system, including the life forms upon planet earth, is thought to be made of this star debris. Thus has arisen the poetic generalization that we are all "made of stardust" and are therefore "one with the universe." This false idea fits in well with the New Age movement, a satanic activity of our day. Man—in the form of Adam—was indeed made from the "dust" of the ground. However, the earth and its component materials were created *before* the stars, not *from* the stars (Gen. 1:16).

58. What are the southern skies like?

The earth maintains a permanent tilt of its north-south axis as it circles the sun. The angle of this tilt is 23.5°, as can be seen on any classroom globe. As a result, we in the northern hemisphere never get a look at the stars in the far southern skies. Likewise, the North Star cannot be seen by people below the equator. Notable stars in the southern hemisphere include Alpha Centauri, earth's nearest star after the sun, and Canopus, the second brightest star after Sirius. The Southern Cross, which is the smallest constellation in the sky, lies close to the southern celestial pole. Countries "down under" are so proud of this small but bright constellation that several print it on their flags. It is interesting that cross constellations are present in both the northern and southern skies: the Swan (Cygnus) in the north, and the Southern Cross (Crux) in the south. Two fuzzy patches of light are also seen in the southern sky. They mark galaxies of stars called the Magellanic Clouds. These are our nearest galaxies and are 170,000 light-years away. Wherever one travels on planet earth, the land is filled with God's goodness and the skies are filled with his glory!

59. Does everyone see the same stars?

From the perspective of the northern hemisphere, everyone sees roughly the same stars on a given night. If it is December, the winter stars are seen from both North America and from Europe, but one's latitude will determine how high a given star "rises" in the sky. From the southern hemisphere, stars in the far north, such as Polaris and the Big Dipper constellation remain hidden below the horizon. These are replaced by such southern stars as Alpha Centauri and the Southern Cross, which cannot be seen from the northern latitudes.

60. Did a vapor canopy once hide the stars?

The term *vapor canopy* refers to a reservoir of moisture that may have existed in the upper atmosphere from the time of creation until the Genesis flood. Possible biblical references include the separation of waters above and below the "firmament" (Gen. 1:6–7, KJV) and the opening of the "floodgates" of heaven (Gen. 7:11). The canopy is thought to have collapsed at the time of the flood, so there is no direct way to answer the question about its earlier existence. However, we know that water in the form of gaseous vapor (isolated molecules) is invisible and that there is always unseen moisture (humidity) present in the air. Water in the atmosphere becomes visible only when a million or more water molecules join together as fog or cloud droplets. The white "vapor trails" that sometimes appear behind jet airplanes are not really gaseous vapor at all but water drops that form from the aircraft fuel or from the air. When the drops vaporize or dissipate, the "contrail" disappears.

Since, in large quantities, water vapor will absorb and scatter light, the earth's vapor canopy may have once somewhat dimmed the heavenly lights. One technical study concluded that a canopy-covered night sky might have looked the same as a night when a full moon is present. If this is correct, the dim stars would have remained unseen. However, the canopy would certainly not have hidden the sun, moon, or brightest stars. We know from Scripture that from the very beginning, the heavens have served their purpose as lights for the earth, markers for seasons, and reminders of God's great glory.

61. How can we see distant stars in a "young" universe?

This is a frequent question asked in Creation Science. If the universe is only 10,000 years old, how can we see galaxies that are millions or billions of light-years away? Many suggestions have been offered, and some follow, with pertinent comments:

1. *Stars are nearby.* This view holds that all the stars are actually quite close to us, within a few thousand light-years. However, the universe must be much larger than this to hold the vast number of stars we see. The Milky Way galaxy with its 100 billion stars is 100,000 light-years across. And uncounted other galaxies can be seen as dim, distant islands in space. The only alternative to vast size is that these galaxies are some kind of miniature lights nearby. But this is implausible and also opposes the glory evident in the heavens.

2. *Space is curved.* Distant starlight is thought to reach us quickly by taking a "shortcut" along some kind of curved path through space. Curved space is a mathematical concept which is difficult to visualize. Also, the observed distribution of stars in space does not seem to support this idea. It must be realized, however, that we know very little about the geometry of deep space. Almost any mathematical arrangement could be suggested.

3. *Decaying light speed.* If the speed of light was greater in the past, early starlight could have moved more rapidly across space than today (see Question 97).

4. *Mature creation.* The light was created together with the stars and instantly spread out across space.

The fourth suggestion is accepted by many creationists. It is a simple solution and is entirely consistent with the creation account. The Garden of Eden was formed with trees already bearing fruit, and Adam and Eve were created as adults. Similarly, we can conclude that the universe was formed as a fully functioning whole, not in an infant stage.

Consider the alternative: since the nearest star, Alpha Centauri, is about four light-years away, Adam and Eve would not have seen even this star for the first four years. Then the stars would have slowly blinked on, one by one. Yet, the Bible tells us that from the beginning, stars have had the purpose of providing a calendar system (Gen. 1:14). Therefore they must have been visible from the moment of their creation on the fourth day. In our own day, we do not see new stars "turning on" in the night sky, as if their light finally reached the earth. Instead, we can state that starlight was created as part of each star and was present throughout space from the beginning of time.

PART 4

Galaxies and the Universe

62. What is the Milky Way?

Our galaxy, the Milky Way, can be seen in all its glory on clear, moonless nights. Appearing as a diffuse band of glowing light, it stretches across the sky from north to south. The path of soft light looks like a trail of clouds or smoke (except that it doesn't blow away), and the further you are from city lights, the more majestic it becomes. In mythology, the Milky Way was known as a heavenly river that led to the world beyond. American Indians looked at the many stars that shine beside this "river in the sky," and believed that they were the campfires of departed warriors.

Galileo, in 1610, was the first to view the Milky Way in detail with a telescope. Instead of the fabled celestial river, the glowing band was found to be made up of countless distant stars. The telescope also showed that the heavens were far larger than previously thought. The Milky Way is actually a pancake-shaped cluster of stars. There is a bulge in the center where the "batter" of stars is extra-thick (see figure 7).

The outer regions of our galaxy are thought to have the shape of spiral arms. The details are uncertain, simply because we live *inside* the Milky Way and cannot get a look at our galaxy from the outside! The best information comes

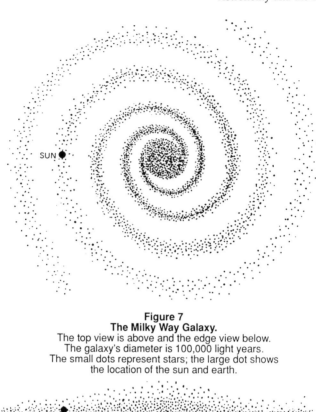

Figure 7
The Milky Way Galaxy.
The top view is above and the edge view below.
The galaxy's diameter is 100,000 light years.
The small dots represent stars; the large dot shows
the location of the sun and earth.

by looking beyond the Milky Way toward other galaxies. Then we see the delicate pinwheel shape of other vast islands of stars.

The Milky Way consists of a hundred billion stars. If divided up, there would be dozens of Milky Way stars for every person on earth! If one could travel across the span of our galaxy at the speed of light, the time required would be 100,000 years. The distance traveled would be 600,000 trillion miles. Such numbers quickly become even more incomprehensible than the federal deficit!

The earth is located about two - thirds of the way out

toward the outer edge of the Milky Way. Instead of living in the bright central hub, we are in a spiral arm, "out in the countryside" of the galaxy. To visualize this, consider a penny as a model of the Milky Way. Planet earth would then be placed inside the circle of the "9" in the date. Also inside this small circle would be the other planets, the sun, and all the stars we can see. The stars of the night sky are visible only because they are very close to us. Distance and obscuring dust prevent us from seeing the remaining 99 percent of the Milky Way galaxy. Here is another illustration of size: if the solar system were as small as a coffee cup, the Milky Way would be the size of North America!

Far beyond the Milky Way, other galaxies of stars seem to extend forever. Astronomers have named a few of them: Andromeda, Magellanic Clouds, the Whirlpool galaxy. There is even one called Snickers. The grand total of the multitude of stars in all the galaxies is immense. The number closely matches estimates of the grains of sand on all the seashores (Question 91). And every star is a sun, a vast reservoir of heat and light. The study of galaxies certainly teaches a lesson about man's smallness and God's glory.

63. Is the universe expanding?

Measurements indicate that the universe may be continually expanding, or spreading out. The most distant galaxies and quasars seem to have departing speeds that are close to the speed of light. The evidence is based on the red-shift of light. If a light source such as a galaxy is moving away from the earth, there will be a shift toward the longer wavelength end of the spectrum, that is, in the direction of red-colored light. This shift is noticed for nearly all of the galaxies beyond the Milky Way. Such galaxies don't actually turn red, but their spectra reveal the shift of their wavelength toward red.

The red-shift of starlight is often taken as evidence for

the Big Bang theory (see next two questions). Yesterday the universe was a bit smaller than it is today, and it was even smaller a year ago. By this backward extrapolation, the universe is hypothetically contracted to a point of explosion, 10 to 15 billion years ago. It must be noted that extrapolation can be a dangerous practice in science, for two reasons in this case. First, a guess must be made concerning rates of change in the past. When God placed the stars in the sky, there was *instant* expansion! Therefore, present rates of change should *not* be used to try to interpret the past. Second, extrapolation may not be taken beyond the actual beginning point. If the universe is 10,000 years old, that must be the limit of extrapolation. Expansion of the universe is just one possible explanation for the red-shift of starlight (see Question 66). If this theory is correct, God surely has his own purposes for creating a universe in outward motion. Perhaps it provides stability: in a static universe, gravity would eventually cause all galaxies to collapse inward.

64. What is the Big Bang theory?

The "big bang" is a popular, secular explanation for the origin of the universe. The theory will be outlined here without commenting on its problems and deficiencies. The process supposedly began with the explosion of a nugget, or "kernel," of mass energy, about fifteen billion years ago. As the energetic radiation spread outward, temperatures slowly cooled enough for hydrogen and helium atoms to form. About ten billion years ago, the first stars began to form from the cooling gas in the young universe. This star-forming process eventually gave rise to the Milky Way and other galaxies. When these initial stars had sufficiently aged, some of them became supernovae explosions. The resulting star fragments later recombined into new stars to repeat the formation-disintegration process. Our sun is said to be a third-generation star, a relatively recent addition to the family of stars, and to have formed around five billion years ago. Other star fragments are thought to provide the material for planets and life forms, including people. Figure 8 is a brief summary of the Big Bang theory.

One modification of this story is called the Oscillating Big Bang theory. This is an attempt to avoid having to explain the initial event. Any unexplained origin is embarrassing to science, even if it is only an explosion! According to this theory, the oscillating universe ceases to expand after a while and begins to fall back on itself. Gravity pulls everything in toward the original kernel of mass energy. Any record of the prior universe is eventually burned and destroyed completely. The kernel then re-explodes outward, and a new universe begins. The time period between the "big bangs" is estimated at forty billion years. The theory of a self-generating, oscillating universe is similar to ancient Greek ideas of eternal cycles. It is convenient to secular thinking because an oscillating universe avoids both a definitive origin and a final destiny for all matter, both living and non-living.

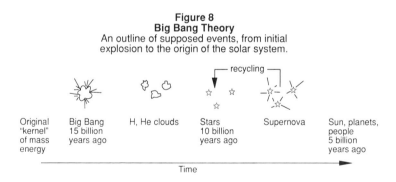

Figure 8
Big Bang Theory
An outline of supposed events, from initial
explosion to the origin of the solar system.

65. *Was* there a Big Bang?

The Big Bang is usually defined as a random, chance event. As noted in the previous question, some instability supposedly developed in an original "kernel" of mass energy, and the universe ballooned outward. However, Scripture clearly rules out such an accidental origin. A modified version of the Big Bang theory says that when the explosive event happened, it was directed by God. This is the theistic-evolution approach, an attempt to compromise the Bible with evolutionary theories, and it, too, must be rejected because of its many conflicts with the order of events in Genesis. Table 6 contrasts some of the chronological discrepancies between the Bible's creation account and the Big Bang hypothesis.

Creationists maintain that what really happened at the time of creation is that God spoke and the earth appeared—he commanded and the heavens stood firm (Ps. 33:9)! All the many stars appeared suddenly and supernaturally in space. Scripture does not imply an explosion, although the universe must have experienced a sudden "explosive" input of ordered energy. Perhaps some of the astronomical data that seems supportive of the Big Bang theory, such as redshift and background radiation, needs to be looked at instead as evidence of a rapid creation. One secular variation of the Big Bang theory refers to an "inflationary" Big Bang, the suggestion being that the universe developed and matured very quickly in its first moments. In this particular theory, secular science seems to have taken one step in the

Table 6 **Chronological Discrepancies Between Scripture and Big Bang**

Scripture	Big Bang
All elements made together	Elements beyond hydrogen and helium formed after millions of years
Earth formed before stars	Earth formed long after stars
Plants formed before the sun	Plants evolved after the sun
Sun formed on the fourth day, after the earth	Sun formed before the earth
Sun, moon, and stars formed together	Sun formed from older stars

creationists' direction. Further developments should be of interest in this area of theory and research.

The Big Bang as it is understood today is an inadequate theory since there are many fundamental problems that are seldom mentioned in the pertinent literature. The following are some "missing links" in the theory:

1. *Missing Origin.* The Big Bang theory assumes an original concentration of energy. Where did this energy come from? Astronomers sometimes speak of origin from a "quantum mechanical fluctuation within a vacuum." However, an energy source is still needed. Actually, there is *no* secular origin theory, since every idea is based on pre-existing matter or energy.

2. *Missing Fuse.* What ignited the Big Bang? The mass concentration proposed in this theory would remain forever as a universal black hole. Gravity would prevent it from expanding outward.

3. *Missing Star Formation.* No natural way has been found to explain the formation of planets, stars, and galaxies. An explosion should produce, at best, an outward spray of gas and radiation. This gas should continue expanding, not form intricate planets, stars, and entire galaxies.

4. *Missing Antimatter.* Some versions of the Big Bang theory require an equal production of matter and antimatter. However, only small traces of antimatter (positrons, antiprotons) are found in space.

5. *Missing Time.* Some experiments indicate that the universe may be young, on the order of 10,000 years old. If true, then there is not sufficient time for the consequences of the Big Bang to unfold. A short time span would not allow for the *gradual* evolution of the earth, heavens, and mankind.

6. *Missing Mass.* Many scientists assume that the universe will eventually stop expanding and begin to collapse inward. Then it will again explode, and repeat its oscillating type of perpetual motion. This idea is an effort to avoid an

origin and destiny for the universe. For oscillation to occur, the universe must have a certain density or distribution of mass. So far, measurements of the mass density are a hundred times smaller than expected. The universe does not appear to be oscillating. The necessary mass is "missing."

7. *Missing Life.* In an evolving universe, life should have developed everywhere. Space should be filled with radio signals from intelligent life forms. Where is everybody?

8. *Missing Neutrinos.* These small particles should flood the earth from the sun's fusion process. Their absence raises questions about the sun's energy source and man's overall understanding of the universe. How then can science speak about "origins" with any authority?

66. How is red-shift explained?

The red-shift of starlight is a decrease in the energy of the light. This energy decrease results in a lengthening of the wavelength of the light, measured with an instrument called a spectrometer. Red is the rainbow color with the longest wavelength, hence the name "red-shift." Stars do not actually become red in appearance since the wavelength change is usually slight. Almost every star and galaxy is found to be red-shifted. The following list summarizes some of the alternative explanations for the origin of this stellar red-shift.

1. *Stellar Motion.* If a star moves outward from the earth, its light energy will be reduced and its wavelength stretched or red-shifted. Stars and entire galaxies show varying amounts of red-shift, therefore implying a variety of speeds for these objects. Police actually use this same effect with radar to measure the speed of cars. Stellar motion is often taken as evidence in support of the Big Bang theory. Stars are assumed to be speeding outward as a result of the ex-

plosion. This is not the only explanation of red-shift, however.

2. *Gravitation*. As light leaves a star, the star's gravity may slightly lengthen the wavelength of the light. A gravitational red-shift could also result from starlight passing near a massive object in space, such as a galaxy. As the light escapes from a strong gravity field, it loses energy, similar to what happens to a person struggling to the top of a mountain.

3. *Second-Order Doppler Effect*. A light source moving at right angles (tangentially) to an observer will always be red-shifted. This can be observed in the laboratory by using a high-speed turntable. A detector is placed in the center and a gamma radiation source is placed on the outside edge. The gamma energy is seen to decrease, or "red-shift," as the turntable speed increases. This is an intriguing explanation for stellar red-shift. When applied to stars, it implies that the universe may be in circular motion instead of radial expansion.

4. *Photon Interaction*. It is possible that light waves exchange energy during their movement across space and lose some energy in the process. A loss of light energy is equivalent to a "reddening" of its light. A theoretical understanding of this proposed "tired light" process has not yet been developed.

Any of these four explanations, alone or in combination, may be responsible for red-shift. We do not know enough about space to be certain of the source of stellar red-shift.

67. What is background radiation?

A low energy form of the microwaves that permeate space, background radiation was first detected in 1965 by researchers at Bell Laboratories. The radiation has an energy that is equivalent to a temperature of three degrees Kelvin

($-270°$ C, or $-455°$ F, just above absolute zero), which can be considered the overall temperature of space. Background radiation has been made an integral part of the Big Bang theory: it is said that this low energy is the "last dying ember" of the original explosion and that—after 15 billion years—the universe has cooled down to this very low temperature.

The red-shift of starlight and background radiation have become identified as the two main evidences for the Big Bang. Largely because of the hypothesized significance of the radiation, its discoverers received a Nobel Prize in physics in 1970. However, even "scientific" conclusions are not all as certain as they sound. Scientists continue to have trouble matching the radiation's isotropy, or directional nature, with Big Bang predictions. The radiation also shows significant differences from the "black-body spectrum" that the Big Bang theory predicts. For the creationist who rejects the Big Bang theory, there are alternative explanations for the background radiation:

1. It may result from the supernatural creation event.
2. The radiation may be emitted from certain types of stars or entire galaxies. Space is also filled with cosmic rays, whose source is not known.

68. Why does everything in space display circular motion?

God has created a dynamic universe whose contents are in constant motion. *Rotation* is the turning of an object on its axis (like the spinning earth), whereas *revolution* refers to the orbital motion of moons around planets and planets around the sun. Table 7 shows the rotation times for various objects in space. Several items in this list deserve additional comment. *Pulsars* are a category of collapsed stars that spin wildly. Their rotation is observed to slow down very grad-

Table 7 **Rotation Periods for Objects in Space**

Object	Rotation Period
Pulsar stars	.001-1 second
Jupiter	10 hours
Earth	24 hours
Comet Halley	48-168 hours
Moon	29½ days
Sun	28 days
Venus	243 days
Milky Way	225 million years

ually as energy is lost into space. As for the *earth,* rotation provides the obvious day/night cycle. The rotation of *Comet Halley* was roughly determined during its 1986 appearance. The large time value for the Milky Way galaxy does not mean that it is ancient! In the recent-creation view, this galaxy is still in its first rotation. The galaxy's spin rate is not as lazy as it sounds; the entire solar system moves at 500,000 miles per hour around the galaxy. One purpose of the circular motion of all objects in space is to provide stability. If planets and moons did not have orbital motion, gravity would cause them to crash inward. If the Milky Way was a stationary group of stars, then they would also begin moving toward the center. The galaxy's rotation prevents this unstable situation.

69. How old is the universe?

There are many measurements that purportedly give ages for the earth, moon, and stars, but one finds a wide range of estimates, depending on the assumptions of the experiments. At one extreme, details such as moon dust and Saturn rings give a maximum age for the universe of only thousands of years. At the other extreme, radiometric dating of rocks seems to indicate billions of years. One can choose just about any age by selecting a particular exper-

iment or basis of measurement. Even a single experiment
can seemingly yield conflicting results, depending on the
interpretation of the data. Creationists have emphasized the
recent-age measurements, providing a long-needed balance
to the age issue. Many creationists believe that measurements indicating a "young" universe are much closer to the
truth, and that extreme-age data need critical scrutiny. Given
the wide range of suggested age values, it appears unlikely
that scientists will be able to settle the issue. There are too
many variables, unknowns, and biases for there to be
agreement on the age of anything as complex as the universe.

Scripture provides an alternative to the scientific debate
over the age of the earth and the universe of which it is a
part. The Bible is not ambiguous. It promotes a universal
age between 6,000 and 10,000 years, the length of time that
provides a sufficient framework for biblical history. In contrast, the current secular view regarding the age of the
universe is 15 billion years, a time span that is 1.5 million
times *longer* than the Bible indicates.

To force a long time scale on the universe is wrong, for
three reasons. First, it selects just one age view, admittedly
the most popular one, from the many choices available in
science. Second, the figure of 15 billion years is probably
only temporary. As new dating techniques are perfected,
the science establishment may change its estimated time
scale of history to 15 thousand years or even to 15 trillion
years. And where does this open-ended question leave the
unchanging Scripture? Third, the secular view of science
conflicts with Scripture in many details, the most important
of which include creation versus evolution, and purpose
versus randomness in the universe.

70. What is a quasar?

Quasars are mysterious sources of distant light. The name
stands for "quasi-stellar" objects. Since their discovery in

1962, hundreds of quasars have been detected with telescopes. They have been variously identified as exotic stars, exploding galaxies, and even black-hole collisions. The main distinction of quasars is an extremely large red-shift of their light. This would seem to imply an outward motion of the quasars in space, and at very high speeds. They are also thought to be the most distant objects we have observed (perhaps 15 billion light-years away). This raises the question of how we can "see" objects that are so far away, since their actual brightness would therefore have to be tremendous. Because of this brightness problem, a few astronomers have begun to doubt the standard view that quasars are extremely remote objects in the universe. They believe that quasars are actually quite close to us, perhaps within our own Milky Way galaxy, and that their brightness is "normal." If this is true, there must be some other explanation for the measured red-shift, besides extreme speed and distance (see Question 66). In fact, quasars may hold the key to a basic understanding of the size and motion of the physical universe.

71. Is heaven located in the northern sky?

This recurring idea has apparent support from Job 26:7: "He [God] spreads out the northern skies over empty space. . . ." Although some Bible students have taken this verse to indicate a significant direction in space, perhaps the location of heaven, the reference more likely refers to the broad northern expanse in general. This particular direction may have been emphasized because of the apparent motion of all other stars around a stationary point in the north sky (presently Polaris) that results from the earth's rotation. An "empty space," devoid of stars, is not found in the north. Instead, billions of stars and galaxies extend outward in all directions. Although heaven is a literal place, it has not been seen with telescopes. It may indeed exist in the northern direction, or in a distant region of the universe, or in another dimension altogether. Scripture indicates that heaven may exist entirely beyond the visible universe. In 2 Corinthians 12:2–3, the apostle Paul refers to "the third heaven"—paradise—far beyond the first heaven (earth's atmosphere) and the second heaven (the realm of the stars). He also speaks of the Lord's having "ascended higher than all the heavens" (Eph. 4:10).

PART 5

General Science

72. What is gravity?

Gravity is a force of attraction that exists between all objects. For example, the earth's gravity keeps the moon in orbit; the moon pulls back and causes the tides. The earth also pulls downward and gives objects their "weight." On the moon you would weigh six times less than on earth, because lunar gravity is less than earth's. Gravity acts through the vacuum of space and is the only force strong enough to extend like invisible cords through vast distances.

On earth, gravity causes the rain to "fall." It also makes us tired, since we work against its force all day. Gravity cannot be turned off: no anti-gravity machine has yet been invented. To experience the weightlessness they will encounter in space, astronauts often train in pools of water. A few moments of artificial weightlessness can also be produced in an airplane that is flown in a loop. (Perhaps you recall the feeling from a roller coaster ride.) It is fun to think about what life on earth would be like if gravity was stronger than it actually is:

Ink would drain from your pen.

No birds or planes could fly.

No tall trees or buildings could stand.

Neither evaporation nor rain would occur.

Clouds would lie on the ground.

Standing up would be a difficult task.

Or consider the opposite, a weakened gravity force:

We would weigh less.

A home-run baseball would fly for miles.

Earth's atmosphere would escape into space.

Oceans would evaporate.

Clearly, God has given gravity the correct strength to make life possible on earth. Isaac Newton studied gravity three centuries ago, but modern science still does not know what really causes its force. What an incredible mystery! How do the earth and moon "know" exactly where the other is at all times and pull accordingly? Some have guessed that invisible gravity particles stream between objects like strands of glue. Of course, we can write equations for gravity, but they are just imperfect descriptions. Whatever the mechanism, God upholds the force of gravity by his power (Col. 1:16–17; Heb. 1:3). Even those people who fail to acknowledge the God who establishes natural laws learn to accept the law of gravity through experience. How much richer to know both the law *and* the law-giver!

73. What is light?

Simple questions in science often have complicated answers, and light is an excellent example. Light has both particle-like properties and wave properties. That is, light sometimes behaves like invisible particles called *photons*.

These photons can collide with other particles such as electrons, and be deflected like microscopic marbles. At the same time, light also displays wavelengths which can act similar to water waves or sound waves. Scientists accept this unusual dual nature of light without completely understanding it.

We are familiar with visible light, of course. The sun produces the dramatic colors that brighten our day. Rainbows, blue skies, red sunsets—all result from the separation of sunlight into its spectral colors. However, this visible light is only a small part of the total picture. The sun and other stars also emit many kinds of light that our eyes cannot see. You have heard of some of these forms of light: radio waves and microwaves, ultraviolet and infrared, x-rays and gamma rays. All of these strange varieties of light flood our sky continually. If we could see them, the heavens would appear to be bright with energy. Although this sounds dangerous, it should be noted that the microwaves from space are just a whisper, much weaker than those produced inside a microwave oven. Also, most of the ultraviolet and x-rays are safely absorbed by the earth's atmosphere. In recent years, instruments have been designed to detect and learn from these invisible kinds of light. For example, infrared telescopes show us many new details of stars and galaxies, and receivers for the radio waves are built in the form of huge dishes. There is obviously much more light in space than "meets the eye," and each variety of light, visible or invisible, has its own story to tell about the heavens.

Light was part of the initial creation, the opposite of darkness (Gen. 1:3). God is called "light" (1 John 1:5) and "Father of the heavenly lights" (James 1:17). This is a fitting title because light is pure, beautiful, and beyond human understanding. Christians are expected to be part of this image, since we are told to let our light "shine before men" (Matt. 5:16).

74. What is a light-year?

This term is misleading, because a light-year measures distance, not time. Many units of distance have been defined in science, and the light-year is one of the longest. It is equal to the distance that a beam of light travels in one year. The speed of light is usually given the symbol c, and can be written as c = 186,000 miles/second (or 300,000 kilometers/second). The length of a light-year is 5.58×10^{12} miles, or roughly 6 trillion miles (about 10 trillion kilometers). This vast distance is equivalent to about 12 million round trips to the moon. A light-year is also the approximate total distance that all the motorized vehicles on earth travel during the course of a year.

The light-year measurement is useful in describing stellar distances. The closest star to earth (after the sun) is Alpha Centauri, 4.3 light years away. Since this distance is 250,000 times greater than that to the sun, it is obvious that earth is remote and isolated from the stellar heavens. The Voyager spacecraft would take more than 100,000 years to reach Alpha Centauri. Table 8 gives earth's distance to several objects in space.

Table 8 **Distance to Objects in Space**

Object	Distance from Earth
Moon	1.3 light-seconds
Sun	8.3 light-minutes
Pluto	5.3 light-hours
Big Dipper stars	100 light-years (average)
Milky Way, diameter of	100,000 light-years
Andromeda	2 million light-years
Quasars	10 billion light-years

75. What did ancient observatories measure?

Around the world are many ancient stone markers, which were apparently once used to measure the heavens. Since these monuments remain today, they must have been built in the years *following* the Genesis flood. They are found everywhere: England's Stonehenge, Wyoming's Big Horn Wheel, Tonga's Coral Arch. Their common purpose was the determination of the exact change of seasons. In particular, the stone pillars are aligned with the rising and setting of the sun at the time of solstice. In the northern hemisphere, summer solstice occurs around June 21 each year. This is the first day of summer and also the longest day of the year. Each day during the spring the noontime sun has been climbing higher in the sky. At the solstice it makes a turn-around and begins heading back south. The ancients carefully measured this special day when the sun is furthest north and noon shadows are shortest. Six months later, on December 22, is the winter solstice, the southern hemisphere's turn for the longest day. The sun's annual path appears to move back and forth across the equator, between 23.5° North (the Tropic of Cancer) and 23.5° South (the Tropic of Capricorn).

Those impressive stone markers show us how essential having a calendar has been to mankind throughout history. We take our wall calendars and clocks for granted, but early people did not have such luxuries. Rather, they expended great effort in building crude observatories and then carefully watched the heavens. Measurements of objects in the heavens were needed to tell them when to plant crops and when to prepare for winter. According to the Bible, one of the reasons for "lights" in the sky is to provide a reference for days, seasons, and years (Gen. 1:14).

76. What's wrong with studying astrology?

Astrology is a pseudo-science based on the view that the stars and planets exert a strong influence on human affairs. It claims not only that the relative positions of the heavenly bodies at an individual's birth determine his or her basic makeup, but that changing astral positions can be used to predict the future. However, because the heavens were never intended for that purpose, astrology is a dangerous and wrongful practice. Stars were created for calendar keeping and for declaring God's glory. To use them otherwise is idolatry, as warned against throughout Scripture (Deut. 4:19; 2 Kings 23:5; Isa. 47:13b, etc.). Astrology should not even be consulted for amusement. It is connected with the forces of evil and can lead to occult practices and bondage to sin.

Astrology has three major flaws, each of which cancels any claim to scientific validity. First, astrology fails to succeed when tested against reality. For example, the distribution of the heavens at the moment of birth is supposed to determine one's astrological sign and thus one's personality and future. On that basis, twins should have nearly identical lives. However, twins often vary greatly in talent, personality, and the paths of life they choose. Remember Jacob and Esau! Second, one's so-called astrological sign is no longer valid. Because of the precession of the earth's axis (Question 42), a person is actually born under a different star sign than is assigned to him by the outdated horoscopes still in use today. Astrology is based on the *former* positions of stars (as they were three thousand years ago, in Babylonian times). Each year, the error in dating the zodiac signs grows greater. Third, it is impossible for the stars to have an effect on a person, much less on worldly events. The gravity of stars and planets is the only force that acts through space distances, and their effect is negligible on earth.

77. Should man be in space?

Before man first walked on the moon, some people warned that we would fail in the attempt. They based this on the claim that man was created to live only on the earth and that therefore God would not let him conquer space to that degree. History has shown this well-meaning prediction to be false, for—instead of failure—the lunar program (and those that followed) was successful and revealed many new details about God's universe. Space exploration continually shows how beautiful the earth is in comparison with other bodies in space. Of course, secular science does not emphasize that point, but the testimony is nevertheless clear. For the Christian especially, every new space probe has reinforced this Bible-based appreciation of God's creation. Instead of opposing space research, it would seem that the believer has the most to gain. After all, we know that the universe is not here by chance or accident. Instead, there is design and planning in every single detail. The heavens were made for all mankind to enjoy, not for secular science to dominate.

Space exploration itself is acceptable and is in many ways similar to traveling beneath the sea. The deeper we go, the more beautiful are the glories of God's creation. Although the Bible says that God has given the earth to man, but the heavens are the Lord's (Ps. 115:16), this should not be taken as a "no trespassing" sign for the heavens. The earth where God put us is his as well, including everything in it (Ps. 24:1). Space travel is not forbidden in Scripture, but the earth will always be man's home, even during the developing space age. The planets and moons are such very hostile worlds that the visitor to these places must take along essential parts of earth (air, food, fuel) to survive.

The space age has actually been beneficial to the church, especially in missions. For example, computers, a spin-off of space research, are a great aid in Bible translation. Also, satellite communications have made far-flung mission stations much less remote from their sponsors at home. In our day there are increasing opportunities to use technology for worthwhile purposes.

78. What are UFO's?

Unidentified flying objects—UFO's—have several possible explanations. The idea that they bring aliens from another planet is not credible, since no other life form has been discovered in the solar system. Furthermore, the earth is too isolated from all other stars besides the sun to accept the possibility of interstellar visits. There have been rumors that the United States government has secretly collected crashed flying saucers, but these stories are unfounded. Using radio-wave signals, an intense search is being conducted for life in space, and such research is very evolution-oriented. Many scientists believe that life evolved on planet earth and that thus it simply must have evolved elsewhere also. So far, there is no evidence to support this claim (see next question).

A more reasonable explanation of UFO's is that they result from natural events in the earth's atmosphere. For example, clouds sometimes take the unusual form of lenses. These are called *lenticular clouds,* and they have sometimes been mistaken for flying saucers. As another example, certain lightning discharges form a sphere of glowing plasma that can last for several minutes. This *ball lightning* has been seen to drift through the air and even bounce along the ground. Lenticular clouds and ball lightning are just two of dozens of natural phenomena that we do not understand very well and that also could be sources of UFO reports. The atmosphere is very complicated, which is the reason why weather forecasting is so unreliable.

Another possible origin of UFO's is the demonic world. The Bible records that Satan is able to deceive men by many schemes and can disguise himself as an angel of light (2 Cor. 2:11; 11:14). Ephesians 6:12 describes the spiritual forces of evil in heavenly realms, and two possible motives for their promotion of UFO stories come to mind. First, Satan may be trying to provide false evidence in support of evolution. After all (as previously mentioned), some people claim that if evolution occurred on earth, it should have also occurred elsewhere. Flying saucers lead naturally to such thinking. A second motive for fostering a belief in UFO's is related to the Rapture of the church. When this biblically predicted disappearance of believers occurs, there will be some difficult explaining to do! Perhaps some sort of UFO kidnapping plot will be popular at that time.

79. Is there life in space?

All efforts to detect life beyond earth have failed so far. The search began with the moon, where astronauts walked during six lunar landings from 1969 through 1972. After it was concluded that the moon was a sterile, lifeless place, the search moved to the other planets and their moons. Viking probes to Mars in 1976 performed experiments designed to detect life, including microscopic organisms, with negative results. Two unmanned Voyager craft—whose destinations include Jupiter, Saturn, and Uranus—have taken thousands of pictures of the outer solar system. They reveal harsh, nonlivable conditions everywhere (see Question 23). Searches of deepest space have been carried out by radio telescopes, instruments that are able to beam messages of greeting toward any planets that might be circling distant stars. Radio telescopes also "listen" for any space messages that may be coming in earth's direction. During the past few decades, scientists have searched dozens of nearby stars for intelligible radio·signals. The results are once again completely negative. At this point, it appears that life as we know it is unique to planet earth. This conclusion has been very upsetting to evolutionists, who believe that life began spontaneously on earth and that the same thing probably happened elsewhere in the universe.

80. Does Scripture refer to life in space?

The Bible records that spirit beings, both good and evil, are to be found in space. Ephesians 6:12 refers to "spiritual forces of evil in the heavenly realms," and Daniel 10:12–13 gives us a glimpse of the warfare that goes on in high places. Selected Scripture verses are sometimes also quoted in support of *physical* beings in space as distinct from the spirit world:

> "Even if you have been banished to the most distant land under the heavens, from there the LORD your God will gather you" (Deut. 30:4).
>
> " '. . . and the multitudes of heaven worship you' " (Neh. 9:6).
>
> "In that day the LORD will punish the powers in the heavens above . . ." (Isa. 24:21).
>
> "And he will send his angels and gather his elect from the four winds, from the ends of the earth to the ends of the heavens" (Mark 13:27).
>
> "I have other sheep that are not of this sheep pen. I must bring them also . . ." (John 10:16).

It is important to notice that several of these references could well refer to angels. The verses could also describe different groups of people on the earth! Therefore, they are not clear evidence of extraterrestrial life. In contrast, Scripture in general indicates the uniqueness of earth as a sustainer of life:

> "The highest heavens belong to the LORD, but the earth he has given to man" (Ps. 115:16).
>
> ". . . he who fashioned and made the earth, he founded it; he did not create it to be empty, but formed it to be inhabited . . ." (Isa. 45:18).

81. Do eggs balance on the days of the equinox?

First we need some background for this unusual question: There are two days each year when the sun crosses the equator, around March 21 and September 21. At the March equinox, the sun is moving north and spring begins in that hemisphere. The southern hemisphere enters its fall season at the same time. This occasion is called the *vernal equinox,* named for the reawakening of plant life (in the north) and the equal periods of daylight and darkness that occur everywhere on earth. Six months later, the hemispheres' seasons will reverse as the sun again crosses the equator, this time headed south (*autumnal equinox*).

There is a popular idea that eggs behave strangely on the days of the equinox. With the sun above the equator, gravity forces are said to be "in balance," and it is supposedly easy to stand an egg on either end. Try the experiment for yourself. To be thorough, you should also attempt to balance an egg at other times, especially around June or December when the sun is most distant from the equator. Is there any scientific basis to the egg-balancing story? No!

Actually, the sun's gravity force could not "pull upward" on an egg as suggested. A person standing next to an egg produces a "pulling" gravity force 50,000 times greater than the sun, but even this force has a negligible effect on the balancing of an egg. A steady hand can indeed make an egg balance, but it has nothing to do with the equinox. Perhaps the story is connected with Easter eggs and their ancient symbol for spring and rebirth.

82. Is Proctor & Gamble's symbol Satanic?

This rumor is entirely false and has been harmful to the witness of the gospel as well as unfair to Proctor & Gamble. This moon-star symbol was used by the company on many of its products from 1882 to 1985. In figure 9 the stars stand for the thirteen original American colonies, and the drawing is a company logo and nothing more. During the 1960s, a story began circulating that the corporation was controlled by Satan worshipers.   The arrangement of stars in

Figure 9
The Proctor & Gamble logo

the symbol was said to secretly spell out the Revelation 13:18 "number of the beast": 666. Without examining the facts, many people signed petitions against Proctor & Gamble and boycotted their products. Although the story is untrue (Proctor & Gamble is owned by stockholders, not some sinister cult of moon worshipers!), the company dropped the symbol from its products in 1985, so exasperating were the false accusations and bad publicity that the logo had caused. The story continues to be circulated, mainly by misguided Christians. It is a sin to "give false testimony" (Exod. 20:16), and this rumor should not be encouraged by the faithful.

83. What is the strangest word in astronomy?

This distinction probably goes to the word *syzygy*, which refers to a lineup in space of three objects, such as the earth, moon, and sun (see Question 16). This particular alignment occurs twice a month, during new moon and full moon phases. Syzygy is the direct transliteration of a Greek word that appears just once in the New Testament. In Philippians 4:3, the apostle Paul uses *Syzygus* as a title for someone at Philippi, and the word is usually translated as "true yokefellow." Paul was addressing someone who was a companion and fellow worker and was thus "lined up" with

Paul's ministry, similar to how the word *syzygy* is used in modern astronomy. Bible commentaries propose that the original Syzygus was a pastor at Philippi, a friend, or even Paul's wife.

84. How is the date for Easter determined?

You have probably noticed that the date for Easter varies considerably from one year to another. This date comes from a formula established by Constantine the Great and the Council of Nicaea (A.D. 325). You can use the formula to verify the date for Easter each year. First, find the vernal equinox, or first day of spring (about March 21), on a calendar that lists basic astronomical data. Then look for the next full moon, usually indicated in a corner box of the calendar. Easter will fall on the following Sunday. According to the rule, the latest possible date for Easter is April 25, next occurring in 2038. The earliest is March 22, in 2285. Most often, Easter comes during the first week of April. For merchants, the changing date of Easter is inconvenient for annual planning. However, it is pleasing to realize that this special day is not determined by man, but by the movements of the sun and moon. This agrees with the divinely ordained purpose of heavenly lights as markers for times and seasons (Gen. 1:14).

85. Are there limits to science?

There definitely are limits to what science can achieve, as confirmed both in Scripture and in the scientific method. Jeremiah 31:37, for example, clearly implies that there are physical boundaries to what is discoverable by man: "[The Lord says:] 'Only if the heavens above can be measured and the foundations of the earth below be searched out will I reject all the descendants of Israel.' " What this passage is saying is that only *if* all of nature could be perfectly understood by man, would God's promises fail. Because every scientific discovery leads to several new questions God's promises are secure. In general, man creates more problems than he solves! True to God's word in Jeremiah, the interior of the earth remains beyond direct inspection by scientists. The earth has a radius of roughly four thousand miles, while the deepest exploratory wells can reach only about eight miles, or 0.2 percent of the total distance. The internal pressure and temperature of earth are too severe for deeper study. We have not even drilled through the crust, let alone the mantle or core, which explains why such phenomena as the mechanism of the earth's magnetism remain poorly understood. Most of our information on the earth's interior comes from the surface study of vibrations during earthquakes. The Jeremiah passage also implies that the dimensions of the universe cannot be measured. Indeed, we see no end to space and have no way to travel to its extremes. This may be the space age, but the farthest depths of space and their secrets remain far beyond us. The following are some other scriptural references to the limitations of science:

Scientists will never change the seasons or the cycle of day and night (Gen. 8:22).

God does great things beyond our understanding (Job 37:5).

Man cannot alter the motions of the heavens (Job 38:31–33).

The human mind cannot know all there is to know (Col. 2:3).

"Scientific method" is a term describing the experimental approach to pursuing knowledge. A problem is stated, measurements are taken, results are interpreted, and conclusions are drawn. This is an unending process of refinement, but final and absolute truth can never be found scientifically. As new data is discovered, equations and conclusions must be modified to fit the changing picture. Most changes are minor refinements, but some are major scientific breakthroughs, such as relativity and quantum theory. Since only God perfectly understands his creation, man's models and equations about nature are imperfect at best. Many areas, such as origins, miracles, and the spirit world, cannot be understood by secular science at all. Such topics are beyond the capabilities of the scientists and the laboratories in which they labor.

86. Can astronomy lead a person to God?

The heavens bear witness to the glory of God, and Romans 1:20 states that anyone who ignores the testimony of creation does so "without excuse." Unfortunately, many people are not spiritually impressed with the lessons of God's handiwork. Nor are they convinced by fulfilled prophecy or archaeological discoveries, both of which verify at least some of the details of Scripture. Although such evidences are sufficient to make people accountable, they are often not effective in changing lives. The problem is not with the evidence, but with the fact that fallen human nature is blind and irrational. When people turn away from God, their understanding is "darkened" (Rom. 1:21). How else to explain why anyone would turn instead to secular humanism or to the occult?

Theologians use the term *apologetics* for the defense of the truth of Scripture. The view expressed in the previous paragraph is called presuppositional apologetics. That is, the existence of God and the inerrancy of Scripture must be accepted on faith since these truths cannot be scientifically proven in a way that will convince the skeptic. A contrasting view is called evidentialist apologetics, which holds that man *can* be intellectually convinced of spiritual truths. In other words, conversion will follow, once the person has been overwhelmed with the evidence. Thomas Aquinas (1225–1274) promoted this latter view with his rationalism and scientific "proofs" of the existence of God. However, his acceptance of geocentricity is a reminder that his science was fallible. The cruel inquisition that Aquinas supported shows that the intellectual, evidentialist approach to apologetics does not necessarily lead to either understanding or agreement and harmony.

What, then, will bring one to a personal knowledge of the Lord? ". . . faith comes from hearing the message, and the message is heard through the word of Christ" (Rom. 10:17). Of course, prayer is effective in increasing one's understanding, as is the example of a consistent Christian life. Although astronomy and other scientific study of the wonders wrought by the Creator can point one's mind in the right direction, the truth of the Word must come also through the heart.

87. Are there heavenly signs of the End Times?

Scripture contains several prophecies of the changes that will occur in the sky during the final days of this present world. Table 9 presents a summary of these events. Isaiah 51:6 adds that the heavens "will vanish like smoke," and 2 Peter 3:10 states that they "will disappear with a roar." We must conclude from all these biblical predictions that the present universe is only temporary. Signs in the heavens will be part of the final events on earth. In our day, the sun, moon, and stars are very faithful lights, though they are all subject to the aging process.

Since the heavens have always been counted on for stability, dramatic changes in the sky will surely bring terror to many people of that future day. However, the Christian, who knows the Creator of the stars, has no cause to fear such signs. In Jeremiah 10:2, the Lord says, "Do not be

Table 9 **Heavenly Signs of the End Times**

	Isa. 13:10; 34:4 Day of the Lord	Joel 2:10, 31 Day of the Lord	Matt. 24:29, 35 Second Coming	Rev. 6:12–13 Sixth Seal	Rev. 8:10–12 Third and Fourth Trumpets
sun	darkened	darkened	darkened	black	one-third dark
moon	no light	dark, turned to blood	no light	blood red	one-third dark
stars	dissolved, no light	no light	fall	fall	one-third dark, Wormwood star falls
heavens	rolled up like a scroll	tremble	shake, pass away	recede like a rolled-up scroll	

terrified by signs in the sky." A century ago, in England, there occurred what has come to be called the "dark day." Unusual atmospheric conditions led to a day that remained so dark that there was widespread fear and panic about the possible arrival of the world's end. A British government assembly was in session at this time. A suggestion was made that the assembly adjourn so the men could return to their homes. One of the members then stood and made a profound statement that settled everyone down. He said that if the world was indeed at an end, it was too late to rearrange one's life. And if it was not ending, there was work to be done. The men immediately returned to the work at hand. This philosophy of life works well for the Christian. First, be sure that your life is in order before God. Then redeem the time and work for him, instead of standing around and fearfully waiting for signs in the sky.

88. Can the "music of the spheres" be explained?

This phrase is sung in the well-known hymn "This Is My Father's World" by M. D. Babcock (1858–1901): "All nature sings, and 'round me rings / The music of the spheres." The idea was first used in early Greek times. It refers to music that the heavenly bodies were thought to produce as they moved across the sky. The astronomer Johann Kepler (1571–1630) not only emphasized this heavenly music, but even calculated the musical notes that the planets represented.

The idea of celestial tones has a valid basis, since musical notes are always produced by repeated, regular vibrations—whether originating from vibrating strings, reeds, or drum membranes. Human ears are sensitive to vibrations in the range of hundreds to thousands of cycles per second. As the planets circle the sun, the motion of each one is a unique form of slow, regular vibration. The earth's musical frequency is an ultra-bass note of one cycle per year! The frequencies of the other planets fall on either side of this value, although all are far beyond our threshold of hearing. Furthermore, there is no air in outer space to carry the distant sound waves to our ears. We cannot hear it, but the motion and music of the planetary spheres continues, day after day. Perhaps this pure music is enjoyed by the Creator and his host of angels!

89. What quotes are pertinent for our study?

The statements of certain astronomers have become well-known in that they represent the thinking of groups in the scientific community. The following collection of statements by philosophers and scientists is divided into two categories, either supporting or opposing biblical creation. The authors themselves might not agree with the category they have been placed in, but the quotations speak for themselves.

Pro-Creation View

For myself, faith begins with the realization that a supreme intelligence brought the universe into being and created man. It is not difficult for me to have this faith, for it is incontrovertible that where there is a plan there is intelligence—an orderly, unfolding universe testifies to the truth of the most majestic statement ever uttered—'In the beginning God.'

> Arthur Compton (1936)
> *Chicago Daily News*

I suspect that the sun is 4.5 billion years old. However, given some new and unexpected results to the contrary, and some time for frantic recalculation and theoretical readjustment, I suspect that we could live with Bishop Ussher's value for the age of the Earth and Sun. I don't think we have much in the way of observational evidence in astronomy to conflict with that.

> John Eddy (1978)
> *Geotimes*

The details differ, but the essential elements in the astronomical and biblical accounts of Genesis are the same: the chain of events leading to man commenced suddenly and sharply at a definite moment in time, in a flash of light and energy. . . . For the scientist who has lived by his faith in the power of reason, the story ends like a bad dream. He has scaled the mountain of ignorance; he is about to conquer the highest peak; as he pulls himself over the final rock, he is greeted by a band of theologians who have been sitting there for centuries.

> Robert Jastrow (1978)
> *God and the Astronomers*

Now, as God the maker played, He taught the game to Nature, Whom He created in His Image.

> Johann Kepler (1621)
> *The Mystery of the Universe*

This most beautiful system of the sun, planets, and comets, could only proceed from the counsel and dominion of an intelligent and powerful Being.

> Isaac Newton (1687)
> *Principia*

God did not create the planets and stars with the intention

that they should dominate man, but that they, like other creatures, should obey and serve him.

Aureolus Paracelsus (1541)
Concerning the Nature of Things

We believe that God hath made all things out of nothing: because, even though the world hath been made of some material, that very same material hath been made out of nothing.

St. Augustine (A.D. 393)
Of the Faith and of the Creed

Anti-Creation View

I am an atheist, out and out. I don't have the evidence to prove that God doesn't exist, but I so strongly suspect He does not that I don't want to waste my time.

Isaac Asimov (1982)
Context

Contemporary opinion on star formation holds that objects called protostars are formed as condensation from interstellar gas. This condensation process is very difficult theoretically, and no essential theoretical understanding can be claimed; in fact some theoretical evidence argues strongly against the possibility of star formation. However, we know that stars exist, and we must do our best to account for them.

J. C. Brandt (1966)
The Sun and Stars

There is a deep compulsion to believe the idea that the entire universe, including all the apparently concrete matter that assails our senses, is in reality only a frolic of convoluted nothingness, that in the end the world will turn out to be a sculpture of pure emptiness, a self-organized void.

Paul Davies (1984)
Superforce

Even if life is not found in our solar system, there are so many other stars in space that it would *seem* that *some* of them *could* have planets around them, and it would *seem* that life *could* have arisen on *some* of the planets independently of the origin of life on the Earth [italics mine].

> Jay Pasachoff (1981)
> *Contemporary Astronomy*

The cosmos is all that is or ever was or ever will be.

> Carl Sagan (1980)
> *Cosmos*

If any planet has surface conditions suitable or at least tolerable to any terrestrial organisms, life may be assumed to have developed there.

> Carl Sagan and I. Shklouskii (1966)
> *Intelligent Life in the Universe*

In the beginning was the Word, it has been piously recorded and I might venture that the word was hydrogen gas.

> Harlow Shapley (1960)
> *Science Ponders Religion*

It is very hard to realize that this all is just a tiny part of an overwhelmingly hostile universe. It is even harder to realize that this present universe has evolved from an unspeakably unfamiliar early condition, and faces a future extinction of endless cold or intolerable heat. The more the universe seems comprehensible (via the big bang) the more it also seems pointless.

> Steve Weinberg (1977)
> *The First Three Minutes*

PART 6

Technical Terms and Ideas

90. Which is the best telescope to buy?

This is a practical question! Many beginning stargazers become discouraged because they are using the wrong equipment. Just as there are different levels of reference books for the study of Scripture, so there are levels of optical tools for studying the heavens. In both cases, the best advice is to start simply and build upward from that point. One should make quality investments with lasting value. For the beginning astronomer, an initial aid might be binoculars, which should have wide-range optics and a power of about 7. (A label of 7 × 50 means that the magnification is 7, and the aperture or diameter of the front lens is 50 millimeters.) In many ways binoculars are superior to a small telescope. They are easy to use, give excellent views of the moon, planets, and star clusters, and they also work well for *indirect* viewing of solar eclipses and sunspots. *Warning:* The sun's image through binoculars should be projected onto a flat surface so it can be safely studied. After one is familiar with a binocular view of space, a refracting or reflecting telescope can be considered. Seek some informed advice and, if possible, try several out before making a purchase. The initial experiences will help the star-

119

gazer decide which telescope is best for his or her own interests.

91. Are stars as numerous as sand grains?

The promise was given to Abraham that he would be blessed with "descendants as numerous as the stars in the sky and as the sand on the seashore . . ." (Gen. 22:17). What this really means is that the seed of Abraham is beyond count, so one should not look for an exact number of descendants, based on this verse. Still, the numerical comparison between stars and grains of sand provides a good illustration of the vastness of the heavens.

Let us consider a rough estimate for all the sand grains on the seashores of planet earth. We will depict this total as a block of sand that is 10 feet deep, 100 feet wide, and 1,000,000 miles long. This length equals 42 trips around the world, a generous figure for the world's sandy beaches. The total volume of this block is found by multiplying the three

Figure 10
A block of sand, approximately equal
to the world's shorelines.

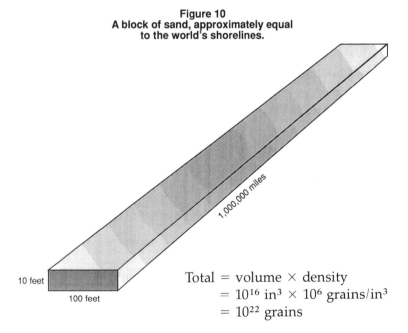

1,000,000 miles

10 feet

100 feet

$$\text{Total} = \text{volume} \times \text{density}$$
$$= 10^{16} \text{ in}^3 \times 10^6 \text{ grains/in}^3$$
$$= 10^{22} \text{ grains}$$

dimensions, which is represented as 5.28×10^{12} ft^3 = 10^{16} in^3. A one-inch cube of average sand contains about 1,000,000 grains (assuming that there are 100 grains lined along each edge). The total number of grains in the imaginary block of sand is depicted in figure 10.

This is the number 1 followed by 22 zeros, which may be expressed as ten billion trillion sand grains. Surprisingly, the very same figure is used to approximate the total number of known stars, including all galaxies! The stars are indeed as numerous as the sands on the seashores. God's children may never reach this number, but his family is large—and growing!

To help us understand vast numbers such as 10^{22}, table 10 lists some other large-number estimates.

Table 10 **Various Large Number Estimates**

Item	Size
Hairs on an average head	2×10^5
Seconds in a year	3×10^7
Retirement age in seconds	2×10^9
World population	5×10^9
Miles in a light year	6×10^{12}
Words spoken since Creation	10^{16}
Sand grains on all shores	10^{22}
Observed stars	10^{22}
Water drops in all oceans	10^{25}
Candle power of the sun	3×10^{27}
Electrons in the observed universe	10^{80}

92. Are relativity and quantum theories correct?

These two fields of study have revolutionized physics during the 1900s. The older science of Isaac Newton's time is called classical physics. The twentieth century has marked the dramatic change from classical to modern physics. Relativity theory refers to the modification of basic equations that is needed when high speeds are involved. As particles move close to the speed of light, their mass, size, speed, and time all behave in the strange new ways predicted by

Albert Einstein's relativity theory. In physics, the term *relativity* basically means that the particles' properties can change relative to the motion. However, for the typical speeds that man uses, even during the space age, classical physics still produces excellent agreement with experimental evidence.

Quantum theory explains how particles interact and exchange energy. It was first formulated by the German physicist Max Planck (1858–1947), yet is very fundamental to science—because we are all made of small particles! a quantum is a tiny amount of energy that cannot be further subdivided. Experiments have shown that energy is always exchanged in these small bundles, or quanta. One troubling part of quantum theory is that some questions in science become unknowable because the exact behavior of atomic particles is unpredictable and unmeasurable. This apparent randomness to nature bothered Einstein greatly. Quantum theory seemed to rule out God's control and foreknowledge of all things. In Einstein's words, he could not believe that "God plays dice with the universe." Einstein believed that all of science should have predictable cause-and-effect results, as it does in classical physics.

Relativity and quantum theories have become foundation stones in modern physics. Hundreds of different experiments seem to verify their correctness. One can always analyze these same experiments within a classical framework, but the results are often forced and complicated. Some scientists continue to reject these theories for philosophical/religious reasons and prefer to interpret modern physics in terms of the older, classical approach. Their efforts are welcome, because they provide checks and balances against possible errors in scientific thinking. However, relativity and quantum theories are elegant and powerful hypotheses. It is certainly rash to limit God by saying that he cannot operate his universe by using these principles or others yet undiscovered. The philosophical problems that seem to arise from relativity and quantum physics may actually be due to mankind's limitations. What appears random or mysterious to us is a certainty to God, who knows *all* things.

93. What is the Anthropic Principle?

This currently popular term in astronomy comes from the Greek word for man, *anthropos*. For any principle of science to be acceptable, there must be experimental results with general validity. The Anthropic Principle which states that the universe is especially suited for the well-being of mankind, is one such assumption. As just one of hundreds of examples, consider the tides that the moon causes on earth. If the moon was closer to the earth, tides would be greatly increased. Ocean waves could sweep across the continents. The seas themselves might heat to the boiling point from the resulting friction. On the other hand, a more distant moon would reduce the tides. Marine life would be endangered by the resulting preponderance of stagnant water! Mankind would also be in trouble because the oxygen in the air we breathe is replenished by marine plants. We can conclude that the moon *is* in the "correct" position for man's well-being. Even such details as the mass of protons and the strength of gravity have values that give stability to the universe and thus reinforce the Anthropic Principle. (Additional examples are given in Question 94.)

The Anthropic Principle is a powerful argument that the universe was *designed*. Of course, whether it is an intricate watch or a beautiful planet, any design plan requires a designer! Evolution theory believes it has an answer to "design" in biological systems by hypothesizing ongoing processes of mutation and natural selection. Living things are said to change very slowly and improve with time. There are many fundamental problems with evolution theory, not the least of which is that—in the case of the Anthropic Principle—the theory provides no answer at all.

Whether describing tides, proton mass, or the earth's position in the solar system, is not a grand design present from the very beginning? These phenomena don't mutate or change with time. The negative response of secular science to new evidences of design is interesting in that it shows the extremes to which man will go to maintain a belief in the random origin of all things. It has even been proposed that there really is an infinite number of universes, each with a completely different set of physical properties. According to such thinking, our particular universe just happens to have conditions suitable for human life, and that is why we are here to enjoy it! Of course, there is no way to detect any "other" universes or comprehend their underlying principles. Scripture describes the creation of just one universe. It contains all things, including the clear marks of the supremely intelligent design of our creator God.

94. What are some examples of the Anthropic Principle?

This scientific principle says that the details of nature are designed for the well-being of man (see Question 93). In other words, the universe is user-friendly! Careful planning has been discovered in nature, and this is a powerful testimony to the Genesis creation account. Two examples will be given here from the hundreds of choices available.

The first example involves the mass of a proton. Although this subatomic particle might at first seem to be of trivial significance, closer inspection reveals that the proton's mass is exactly what is needed to provide both its own stability and that of the entire universe. In contrast, a free neutron (n) (which is a slightly heavier particle) decays into a proton (p), an electron (e), and an antineutrino ($\bar{v}$) with a half-life of just twelve minutes. Thus, $n \rightarrow p + e + \bar{v}$. Free neutrons simply cannot persist in nature. However, if the mass of a proton could be somehow increased by just 0.2 percent, the proton would become an unstable particle and would quickly decay into a neutron, positron (e^+), and neutrino (v). This would be represented as $p \rightarrow n + e^+ + v$. This second reaction does *not* occur, but it *would* if the proton were just *slightly* heavier.

The implications of proton mass are truly universal. Of chief significance is that the hydrogen nucleus is composed of just a single proton. Thus the hypothesized rapid decay of protons would destroy all hydrogen atoms. Furthermore, hydrogen is a major component of not only our bodies but also water molecules, the sun, and all other stars. In fact, hydrogen is the dominant element in the universe. It is obvious that the proton's mass seems to have been wisely planned to be slightly smaller than that of a neutron, in order to prevent the collapse of the universe! Note also that protons are not subject to the influence of mutation or natural selection. We can conclude that their physical properties were chosen from the very beginning and have not changed.

The second design example involves the gravity force. All masses are found to attract each other, with a force that varies inversely as the square of the separation distance between the masses:

$$\text{Gravity Force} \sim \frac{1}{(\text{Separation Distance})^2}$$

Scientists have long wondered about the factor of 2 in this expression. It simply looks "too neat." In an evolved universe, one would not expect such a simple relationship. Why is the distance factor not 1.99 or 2.001? The gravity force has been repeatedly tested with sensitive torsion balances, showing that the factor is indeed precisely 2, at least to five decimal places (2.00000). Any value other than 2 would lead to an eventual catastrophic decay of orbits and of the entire universe. As does the proton mass, the gravity force clearly displays elegant and essential design. Proton mass and gravity strength are just two of the invisible wonders that surround us in the universe. Praise is due the Creator for the delicate details that make possible our very existence in the world he created.

95. What are cosmic strings?

Some astrophysicists believe that there are "superstrings" of mass energy in space. These cosmic strings are said to be invisible and massive and to exist in one to nine different space dimensions. Related theories suggest that these strings may form loops in space, a million light-years in circumference. It is hoped that superstring theory will eventually bring about a unification of all the theories concerning elementary particles and the forces between them. Although some experts boldly predict that a fundamental "theory of everything" will be developed, it is an open question whether cosmic strings will be verified, or instead be replaced by new ideas even more complex. The chief motive behind the superstring theory is to explain how the universe came into being. Whether they know it or not, scientists are searching for the fingerprint of the Creator! Such efforts to understand the universe should be an encouragement for the creationist, who already knows that "The heavens declare the glory of God; the skies proclaim the work of his hands" (Ps. 19:1).

96. Is there a basic building block for matter?

Particle accelerators have been used in studying high-energy physics since the 1930s. Protons are given high speeds and are then directed against targets of various material. The resulting interactions provide a probe of the microscopic world. Large accelerators are now able to achieve penetration of an atomic nucleus, and even to split individual protons and neutrons. What results from these interactions is a shower of more than 150 different "elementary" particles, which exhibit a bewildering array of speeds, masses, charges, and lifetimes. Their names include muons and neutrinos, pions and quarks. Given the hierarchy of ever-deeper levels seen within the atom, one might predict that modern science will never reach the bottom-level building blocks of nature. Instead, the inner layers of complexity seem to continue without any limit. It is like trying to peel an onion; there is always another layer underneath! (see figure 11). Of course, similar layers of complexity are also observed in the heavens above. Such results are to be expected in the work of an infinite Creator.

One consequence of accelerating protons to high-energy levels is to effectively increase their temperature. In this way, physicists are attempting to mimic, on a small scale, the energetic conditions they think existed at the earliest moments of the Big Bang chronology they have proposed. Of course, this interpretation is not essential to particle experiments, even though it gets the most publicity. Alternately, discoveries of the inner atom can be taken to reveal something of the complexity that came into being at the instant of a supernatural creation. Therefore, the creationist need not oppose high-energy experiments, but—on the contrary—can truly enjoy the exciting search for order in nature. As with the stars above, the microscopic details of

Figure 11
Particles of matter in descending order of size.
A proton is one hundred thousand (10^5) times smaller than an atom.

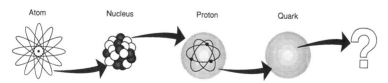

| Atom | Nucleus | Proton | Quark |

God's handiwork are most appreciated by those who know him.

97. Is the speed of light decreasing?

This idea has been suggested by Barry Setterfield of Australia. He believes that the speed of light was infinite at the time of creation but began decreasing at the time of Adam and Eve's sin, when the curse was imposed on nature. Since then, this speed (c) has decayed and slowed to its present value, of c = 300,000 kilometers/second (186,000 miles/second). If true, a changing speed of light could solve a number of the technical problems that creationists must deal with. Since light speed is related to other constants of nature, all the information from radiometric dating would have to be reanalyzed and perhaps shortened. Also, faster light could have traveled from the distant galaxies to the earth very rapidly. Many other findings of science would also be affected by a changing light speed.

Setterfield has examined historical measurements of light speed made over the last three hundred years. He has also looked at the other constants of nature that should have changed in parallel with c. Thus far he has found tentative agreement between the data and his hypothesis of a slowing light speed. However, before creationists give major support to Setterfield's ideas, more study is advisable. In particular, answers are needed to the following questions:

1. Many scientists have looked for evidence of a changing light speed, without success. Why is Setterfield's conclusion different?
2. Early measurements of c are very important in Setterfield's analysis. But isn't the accuracy of early measurements questionable?
3. Setterfield's suggested equation for light decay is very complicated. It includes a logarithm, sine function,

and other constants. Scientific decay formulas usually have a much simpler form.

4. Why did the value of *c* seem to settle down to its present constant value, just when we started to measure it accurately? We cannot see any change in *c* occurring today. This is a suspicious coincidence!

The decay of the speed of light is a revolutionary idea in science. Since many of its implications, both scientific and theological, have not been dealt with, caution is needed in accepting or promoting it. Creationists look forward to the results of further study of this topic.

98. Does the HR Diagram prove that the universe is very "old"?

The HR (Hertzsprung-Russell) Diagram (figure 12) shows the distribution of stars at various surface temperatures and brightnesses. The stars are found to group into three specific categories:

main-sequence stars (1)	"average" stars, such as the sun
red giants (2)	large, bright "cool" stars
white dwarfs (3)	small, dim "hot" stars

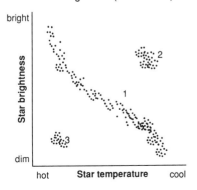

Figure 12
Hertzsprung-Russell Diagram
of Star Distribution
Each data point on the diagram represents a star
with a particular temperature (horizontal axis)
and brightness (vertical axis).

Stellar theory assumes that stars slowly change between these three categories as they age and that each stage of star development lasts for millions or billions of years. Since all three types of stars are seen in abundance in the night sky, secular science concludes that the universe must be ancient.

The creationist has two rebuttals to this idea. First, based on the biblical record, the stars were likely created in all their variety from the very beginning of time: ". . . star differs from star in splendor" (1 Cor. 15:41)—that is in temperature (color) and in brightness. Second, stars may be aging faster than current models suggest. We don't really know the rate of stellar aging, either in the past or in the present.

An HR Diagram can also be drawn for the stars within a particular star cluster. When this is done, one often finds examples of stars that are in an apparent transition stage. That is, their temperature and brightness places them on the diagram between the main-sequence and red giant stars. This pattern is used to promote a multibillion-year age for the clusters. The creationist's reply is once again that the stars are actually all the same age: formed a few thousand years ago when the universe was just four days old. Since then, the more massive stars have probably aged more rapidly and therefore have left the main-sequence category.

99. What is gravitational collapse?

"Gravitational collapse" is proposed by some scientists as an alternate, non-nuclear energy source for the stars (see Question 31). The theory was worked out a century ago by Helmholtz and Kelvin, *before* nuclear energy was discovered. Today, although nuclear fusion is almost universally believed to fuel the stars, detailed studies of the sun have raised serious questions about this assumption. The fusion of hydrogen into helium produces an intense flood of subatomic particles called neutrinos. On that basis, one would expect neutrinos from the sun to reach the earth in vast numbers. However, after years of careful measuring, scientists have simply not detected the expected amounts of solar neutrinos. As a result, a few scientists have begun to doubt that fusion is the dominant energy source for the stars.

The next most likely source of star energy is gravitational contraction. A very slow shrinking of the sun's size would release vast amounts of heat, as the potential energy is converted into kinetic motion of the atoms. A radius shrinkage of just .009 feet/hour or 80 feet/year would produce the total amount of observed solar energy. (Question 32 deals with efforts to measure such a change in the sun's size.) Since this alternate energy source could only supply the sun's energy for a few million years, it has been totally rejected by secular astronomy. This is a case where long-age thinking severely limits the options of science. Perhaps the real source of solar energy is some combination of both gravitational collapse and nuclear fusion.

Gravitational contraction could also be applied to the planet Jupiter, a large planet that is observed to give off more heat than it receives from the sun. A surface contraction of just one centimeter per year would account for the measured heat flow from Jupiter. However, because this change is too small to measure, we do not know whether or not Jupiter is actually experiencing gravitational collapse.

100. Are dying stars a part of the curse in Genesis?

According to the Genesis account, when Adam and Eve sinned, man's relationship with God dramatically changed. Death entered the world through sin (Rom. 5:12), with both spiritual and physical dimensions. The world became a difficult place in which to survive. Genesis 3 describes some of the physical changes that took place, including the growth of "thorns and thistles." From a perfect beginning, life became a struggle; deterioration set in and has been present ever since. Scientists have quantified a law of nature that could be seen as a reflection of God's curse. It is called the Second Law of Thermodynamics, and there are many ways to express it:

> Order in the universe is decreasing.
> Entropy, a measure of disorder, is increasing.
> Energy is becoming unavailable.
> Energy transfer processes are wasteful.
> Everything wears out.

Scripture also describes this aging and decay of all things. Notice that some of the references include the realm of the heavens:

"For, 'All men are like grass, and all their glory is like the flowers of the field; the grass withers and the flowers fall, but the word of the Lord stands forever' " (1 Peter 1:24–25a).

"For the creation was subjected to frustration, not by its own choice, but by the will of the one who subjected it, in hope that the creation itself will be liberated from its bondage to decay and brought into the glorious freedom of the children of God. We know that the whole creation has been groaning as in the pains of childbirth right up to the present time" (Rom. 8:20–22).

"[The heavens] will perish, but you remain; they will all wear out like a garment. Like clothing you will change them and they will be discarded" (Ps. 102:26).

" 'Heaven and earth will pass away, but my words will never pass away' " (Mark 13:31).

" 'Lift up your eyes to the heavens, look at the earth beneath; the heavens will vanish like smoke, the earth will wear out like a garment and its inhabitants die

like flies. But my salvation will last forever, my righteousness will never fail' " (Isa. 51:6).

It seems clear—from both observation and Scripture—that
stars take part in the overall degeneration of the universe.
But is star aging actually part of the "curse"? Were stars
originally intended to shine forever? Several comments can
be made regarding the available options:

1. *If stars originally had the potential to last forever, some
process of perfect energy recycling was needed.* An absence
of the entropic disordering process is difficult to comprehend, but our minds are limited! In a parallel way, partak-
ing of the Tree of Life would have given Adam and Eve
permanent life, yet we cannot understand how a person's
non-glorified physical body could last forever, without
wearing out.

2. *Although the stars of today are temporary, Scripture
seems to indicate permanent stars in the eternal state:*

" 'Those who are wise will shine like the brightness of
heaven, and those who lead many to righteousness, like the
stars for ever and ever' " (Dan. 12:3)

"He set them [stars] in place for ever and ever; he gave a
decree that will never pass away" (Ps. 148:6).

The new, eternal heavens and earth are mentioned in Revelation 21:1. They will surely be very different from the
universe that we know.

3. *Some aspects of the law of entropy must have been in
operation before God's curse* (for example, the eating of fruit
and plants). Similarly, stars (like plants) did not necessarily
take part in the death sentence mentioned in Romans 5:12.
The common terms "dying stars" and "the death of stars"
are perhaps misleading. Stars wear out, but they do not
die in the same way animals do. Stars may have aged from
the very beginning of the creation. We must remember that

the Second Law of Thermodynamics is man's imperfect model of nature's behavior. The actual curse may entail more of nature than the Second Law includes—or maybe less.

4. *Stars were created in great variety: "normal" stars, white dwarfs, and red giants.* This may be part of the internal integrity and consistency of God's universe. A parallel may be found within the Garden of Eden. Trees were surely created with fruit in various stages of development. If all the fruit had been either ripe or unripe, there would have been a food-supply problem for our first parents.

More study is needed concerning the relationship between God's curse and the law of entropy. In both theology and science, many related questions remain unanswered. Meanwhile, an attitude of caution is needed in drawing conclusions in this area. God's ways, including the full implications of his curse, are beyond our understanding. Figure 13 outlines this discussion.

Figure 13
God's curse and the law of entropy.

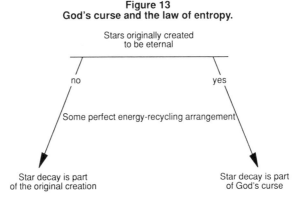

Suggested Resources

General

The Bible and Astronomy, 1984 (John C. Whitcomb, BMH Books, Winona Lake, IN 46590). An excellent introduction to the subject, especially theological truth.

Bible-Science Newsletter (2911 East 42nd Street, Minneapolis, MN 55406). This monthly newspaper is a general resource on Bible-science topics.

Creation Science Magazine (Creation Science Foundation, Ltd., P.O. Box 302, Sunnybrook, Queensland 4109, Australia—American office is at Box 18339, Tucson, AZ 85731). This quarterly magazine takes a clear and colorful look at Bible-science topics. Also called *Ex Nihilo*.

The Earth, the Stars and the Bible, 1979 (Paul B. Steidl, Presbyterian and Reformed Pub. Co., Phillipsburg, NJ 08865). A pioneer effort to interpret astronomy in terms of Scripture.

The Moon-Its Creation, Form, and Significance, 1978 (J. C. Whitcomb and Don DeYoung, BMH Books, Winona Lake, IN 46590). An analysis of the Apollo moon missions in the light of Scripture.

Origins (Geoscience Institute, Loma Linda University, Loma Linda, CA 92350). This biannual journal contains detailed articles and original data on many Bible-science topics.

Origins Research (Students for Origins Research, P.O. Box 203, Goleta, CA 93116-0203). A biannual college newspaper that provides a means for students and educators to critically analyze origins models.

Technical

Creation Research Society Quarterly (P.O. Box 38069, Colorado Springs, CO 80937). Contains research articles that often touch on astronomy. It is the preeminent technical publication in Bible-science.

Design and Origins in Astronomy, 1984 (George Mulfinger, Ed., CRS Books, Norcross, GA 30092). Contains chapters on contemporary topics such as red-shift and cosmology.

Acts and Facts (Institute for Creation Research, P.O. Box 2667, El Cajon, CA 92021). Monthly articles in "Impact" section are on a wide range of Bible-science topics.

Technical monographs published by the Institute for Creation Research and by the Creation Science Foundation of Australia. Addresses are given elsewhere in this section. A collection of detailed studies on specific topics in creationist astronomy.

Glossary

asteroid A "minor planet," smaller than usual planet-size, which orbits the sun.

astrology A nonscientific, cultic system that uses stars and planets to explain human actions.

astronomy The science dealing with the universe and its parts.

aurora Glowing lights in the sky, resulting from space radiation which interacts with the earth's atmosphere.

Big Bang An origin theory which asserts that the universe began explosively from a single point.

black hole A star that has completely collapsed under its own gravity.

comet A mountain-size chunk of frozen matter which orbits the sun. Its orbit alternately brings the comet near to the sun, then to the outer regions of the solar system. When close to the sun, the comet partially melts and develops a surrounding cloud of vapor and a tail. More than 200 different comets have been identified.

creation The supernatural origin of life and matter, brought forth by the Word of God. The word also applies to the present-day universe.

density An object's mass divided by its volume. Density measures the heaviness of matter.

eclipse The movement of one astronomical object into the shadow of another.

element Any of the 109 different kinds of atoms, such as hydrogen, helium, and iron. Ninety-two elements are natural; the rest are manmade and unstable.

evolution The natural, spontaneous origin of life, matter, and the universe.

galaxy A large group of stars, gas, and dust gravitationally tied together. The earth lies within the Milky Way, a spiral-shaped galaxy containing 100 billion stars.

geocentric Centered on the earth.

gravity A fundamental force of nature that results in the attraction of objects. The moon is held captive in its orbit by earth's gravity.

heliocentric Centered on the sun.

light-year The distance that light travels during an entire year if unobstructed. This distance is about six trillion miles.

mass A measure of the total amount of matter in an object.

meteor A streak of light produced when a rock from space, usually fist-sized or smaller, passes through earth's atmosphere and burns. These small objects are often called "shooting stars."

Milky Way *See* galaxy.

moon All natural objects that revolve around planets.

nebula A vast cloud of gas and dust located in space.

nova A star that suddenly increases in brightness.

planet A large object (usually greater than 1000 miles in diameter) which circles a star. Nine known planets orbit the sun. They have no light of their own, but reflect the sunlight.

pulsar A rapidly rotating, dense star. It appears to blink on and off with pulses of light.

orbit The path of the moon as it circles the earth, or the path of the earth around the sun.

quasar Star-like objects which are thought to lie at great distances. Quasar stands for quasi-stellar.

red giant A large star with a relatively cool surface temperature that gives it a red or pink appearance. Red giant stars are one hundred times larger than the sun.

revolution Orbital motion of one object around another. The earth revolves around the sun once each year.

rotation The spinning of an object about its own axis. The earth rotates once each twenty-four hours.

satellite A natural or man-made object that orbits a larger object. The space shuttle and the moon are satellites of the earth. In turn, the earth is a satellite of the sun.

shooting star *See* meteor.

solar system The sun and the surrounding group of objects which orbit around the sun, including planets, asteroids, and comets.

supernova The explosive destruction of a massive star. The explosion is triggered by the collapse of the star when its nuclear fuel is exhausted.

star A giant sphere of gas that averages a million miles in diameter. Its internal temperature is millions of degrees. The sun is an average-size star.

sun *See* star.

velocity A measure of the speed and direction of an object; the distance traveled by an object in a certain time period, divided by the time.

wavelength The distance between wavecrests for any type of wave (water, sound, light).

white dwarf A small, dense, hot type of star. Dwarf stars are one thousand times smaller than the sun.

Scripture Index

Subject Index

Note: References are to question numbers rather than page numbers.